# Essays and Studies 1994

# The English Association

The object of the English Association is to promote the knowledge and appreciation of English language and literature.

The Association pursues these aims by creating opportunities of co-operation among all those interested in English; by furthering the recognition of English as essential in education; by discussing methods of English teaching; by holding lectures, conferences, and other meetings; by publishing a journal, books, and leaflets; and by forming local branches overseas and at home.

## Publications

*The Year's Work in English Studies.* An annual bibliography. Published by Blackwell (U.S.A.: Humanities Press).

*Essays and Studies.* An annual volume of essays by various scholars assembled by the collector covering usually a wide range of subjects and authors from the medieval to the modern. Published by D. S. Brewer.

*English.* The journal of the Association, *English* is published three times a year by the Association.

*Newsletter.* A *Newsletter* is published three times a year giving information about forthcoming publications, conferences, and other matters of interest.

## Benefits of Membership

### Institutional Membership

Full members receive copies of *The Year's Work in English Studies*, *Essays and Studies*, *English* (three issues) and three *Newsletters*.

Ordinary Membership covers *English* (three issues) and three *Newsletters*.

Schools Membership includes two copies of each issue of *English*, one copy of *Essays and Studies*, three *Newsletters*, and preferential booking and rates for various conferences held by the Association.

### Individual Membership

Individuals take out Basic Membership, which entitles them to buy all regular publications of the English Association at a discounted price, and attend Association gatherings.

*For further details* write to The Secretary, The English Association,
The Vicarage, Priory Gardens, London W4 1TT.

## Essays and Studies 1994

# Feminist Linguistics in
# Literary Criticism

Edited by
Katie Wales

for the English Association

D. S. BREWER

ESSAYS AND STUDIES 1994
IS VOLUME FORTY-SEVEN IN THE NEW SERIES
OF ESSAYS AND STUDIES COLLECTED ON BEHALF OF
THE ENGLISH ASSOCIATION
ISSN 0071-1357

First published 1994
D. S. Brewer, Cambridge


ISBN 0 85991 411 9




D. S. Brewer is an imprint of Boydell & Brewer Ltd
PO Box 9, Woodbridge, Suffolk IP12 3DF, UK
and of Boydell & Brewer Inc.
PO Box 41026, Rochester, NY 14604-4126, USA




British Library Cataloguing-in-Publication Data
Feminist Linguistics in Literary Criticism. –
(Essays & Studies 1994,ISSN
0071-1357;Vol.47)
  I. Wales, Katie  II. Series
  801.95
  ISBN 0-85991-441-9

The Library of Congress has cataloged this serial publication:
Catalog card number 36-8431



This publication is printed on acid-free paper

Printed in Great Britain by
St Edmundsbury Press Ltd, Bury St Edmunds, Suffolk

# Contents

Introduction: Feminist Linguistics in Literary Criticism     vii
*Katie Wales*

GENDERED WRITING AND THE WRITER'S     1
    STYLISTIC IDENTITY
*Marion Lomax*

LANGUAGE IN COMMON: APPOSITION IN     21
    CONTEMPORARY POETRY BY WOMEN
*Lesley Jeffries*

WOMEN, MEN AND WORDS: LEXICAL CHOICES IN     51
    TWO FAIRY TALES OF THE 1920s
*Louise Sylvester*

FROM QUEENS TO CONVICTS: STATUS, SEX AND     65
    LANGUAGE IN CONTEMPORARY BRITISH
    WOMEN'S DRAMA
*Anne Varty*

IN DEFENCE OF CELIA: DISCOURSE ANALYSIS AND     91
    WOMEN'S DISCOURSE IN *AS YOU LIKE IT*
*Clara Calvo*

AND THEN HE KISSED HER: THE RECLAMATION OF     117
    FEMALE CHARACTERS TO SUBMISSIVE ROLES IN
    CONTEMPORARY FICTION
*Shan Wareing*

CLOSE ENCOUNTERS OF A FEMINIST KIND:     137
    TRANSITIVITY ANALYSIS AND POP LYRICS
*Sara Mills*

Notes on Contributors     157

# Introduction:
# Feminist Linguistics in
# Literary Criticism

## KATIE WALES

... each/ speaker of the so-called common language feels/ the ice-
flow split, the drift apart/ as if powerless ...

(Adrienne Rich)

THE DIVERSE CONTRIBUTIONS to this collection of seven essays are yet
all united by a common aim. They present an original and close
analysis of a 'literary' text, or range of texts, by applying the methodo-
logy or framework of linguistic (grammatical, lexical, pragmatic, discourse) theories, in order to address directly questions and ideas that
have been raised in feminist literary theory, criticism and linguistics
about gender and style. The volume is not, therefore, yet another
anthology of (previously published) feminist literary criticism: rather,
it is meant to complement such collections. For it tries to show how
feminist literary theory should be put to the practical test, as it were,
under the scrutiny of relevant linguistic insights. The result is a kind
of feminist stylistics, a field which has only recently begun to develop,
and which has considerable potential in the future.[1]

The volume is decidedly eclectic: it ranges in the texts analysed
from Shakespeare's *As You Like it* to present-day pop songs; in feminist
theory from France (Cixous, Kristeva, Irigaray) the United States
(Showalter, Spender) and Britain (Cameron, Coates); and in linguistic models from politeness theory (Brown and Levinson) to transitivity (Halliday). The collection, therefore, very markedly illustrates the
'cross-fertilization' of disciplines and ideas, the lack of which is

---

[1] Feminist stylistics, and indeed, feminist linguistics, is not mentioned in
the survey of feminist criticism by Janet Todd, 'Briefings Number 1: Feminist
Criticism', *The European English Messenger*, 1, no. 2 (Spring 1992), pp.
20–25. Similarly, the survey article on 'Language and Gender' by Janet
Holmes, *Language Teaching*, 24, no. 4 (October 1991), pp. 207–20, with 250
references, only refers to sociolinguistic studies.

lamented by Cameron (1990) in feminist criticism.[2] It is also, very importantly, refreshingly clear of the jargon that tends to pervade both literary and linguistic theory of all kinds. The issues to be tackled, and the 'tools' to be applied, are clearly explained in each chapter for those readers who may not be familiar with them.

There have been several attempts to classify varieties of feminist literary criticism (notably Showalter, 1981),[3] and also feminist linguistics (notably Cameron, 1985);[4] this collection of essays, by reason of its diversity, is therefore difficult to pigeon-hole, like feminist stylistics itself. The analysis of male-authored texts (Shakespeare and Walter de la Mare) in the two contributions by Clara Calvo and Louise Sylvester respectively might be said to belong to 'feminist critique' (Showalter, 1981), except that Calvo is not directly concerned with Shakespeare's 'sexism' or 'sexual politics'; and Sylvester also looks at the comparable fairy tales of Eleanor Farjeon, and so concerns herself with gender difference. Shan Wareing and Sara Mills in their contributions are certainly concerned with questions of sexual politics and the representation of women in popular culture, but the texts involved are mostly written or composed/ performed by women. The remaining three essays, however could certainly be classified as Showalter's 'gynocriticism', since they are precisely concerned with female-authored texts written within a feminist context and consciousness: Lesley Jeffries writing on a range of modern feminist poetry, Marion Lomax on feminist fiction, and Anne Varty on feminist drama. The male perspective is not entirely absent from these chapters (nor the others), since their linguistic models are predominantly male-authored (Grice, Halliday, Quirk et al.). C'est la vie. . . . Nonetheless, the fact that the contributors themselves are all women, even if it is because female academics rather than male are the most interested in feminist stylistics and literary criticism at the moment, means that the presence of a masculine authority appears muted.

---

2 Deborah Cameron, ed., The Feminist Critique of Language: A Reader (Macmillan, London, 1990), p. 27.
3 Elaine Showalter, 'Feminist Criticism in the Wilderness', Critical Inquiry (Winter, 1981), reprinted in E. Abel, ed., Writing and Sexual Difference (Harvester, Brighton, 1982).
4 Deborah Cameron, Feminism and Linguistic Theory (Macmillan, London, 1985).

And, as Eagleton says (1991): 'Men must learn to be silent. This is probably very painful for them'.[5]

Although in this Introduction I do not propose to provide yet another history of the development of either feminist literary criticism/ theory or feminist linguistics, nonetheless I think it is important to identify some of the underlying issues that are the recurring preoccupations of the contributors, and to which they attempt to provide answers. The volume is not meant to be definitive, merely explorative. The essays present plausible interpretations within their own modest limits, sometimes open-ended, because much further research needs to be done. One of the major problems in feminist criticism is that a great deal is said about style and language and gender, but often in broad generalizations. A linguistic-stylistic approach aims to clarify the issues, and test generalizations with concrete evidence from analyses.

One major concern in recent feminist literary theory, as Mills et al. state (1989), is the complex question of gender difference(s) in writing.[6] Potential gender differences in speaking, and language generally, are also an important issue in sociolinguistics and feminist linguistics. The subject is of long-standing interest and very complex; moreover as Coates (1987) emphasizes, befogged with myths and stereotypical assumptions, which still have to be tested in large-scale practical investigations.[7] Moreover, historically at least, the two strands of writing and speaking differences have been considerably confused, and this inheritance has tended to skew early feminist linguistic writing such as Lakoff's (1975) and even possibly écriture féminine, as we shall see.[8] So the influential chapter on women's language in Otto Jespersen's *Language* published seventy years ago in 1922, written from the ideological perspectives of male speech as 'norm' and with positive value, proclaims that women have less extensive vocabularies than men; favour intensifiers like *so* and *such* and vague words like *nice* and *lovely*.[9] Lakoff accepts these comments without question, but

5  Mary Eagleton, ed., *Feminist Literary Criticism* (Longman, London, 1991), p. 5.
6  Sara Mills, Lynne Pearce, Sue Spaull and Elaine Millard, *Feminist Readings/ Feminists Reading* (Harvester Wheatsheaf, London, 1989), p. 4.
7  Jennifer Coates, *Women, Men and Language* (Longman, London, 1987).
8  Robin Lakoff, *Language and Women's Place* (Harper & Row, New York, 1975).
9  Otto Jespersen, *Language* (Allen & Unwin, London). Reprinted in Cameron, ed., op. cit. (1990).

much research needs still to be done on this subject.[10] In this volume Sylvester takes up the challenge declared by Showalter (1981) to address 'lexical ranges' by comparing the precise and similar lexical fields of two writers writing within the same genre at the same period.

Jespersen also states that women use less complex sentence structures, preferring a string of *and*-clauses. Whether Jespersen has speech or writing in mind for this 'feminine period' he does not make clear; nor does he provide any concrete evidence. Co-ordination rather than sub-ordination is a characteristic feature of the speech styles of both sexes; but it is very likely that Jespersen was relying on literature for his generalizations, more precisely, the literary representations of women speaking (Mrs Nickleby, Flora Finching, The Wife of Bath), as rendered by mostly male writers from Chaucer onwards. Behind this 'loose' and hyperbolic style lurk also stereotypical assumptions about female garrulity and scatter-brainedness. Further implications of this, and also of Jespersen's statements, I shall return to below.

By coincidence, in the 1920s also, the subject of the differences between men and women's styles of writing rather than speaking, were being aired by Virginia Woolf, whose criticism generally has been extremely influential on feminist literary criticism. Her statements on gender differences in writing have been frequently quoted; but they are prone to the same generalizing tendency as Jespersen's, and, like any such statements, are in dire need of being empirically tested.

As Lesley Jeffries says in this volume (pp. 21–48), as a reader of texts about women and their relationship with language, 'I want to know what Woolf means by "the woman's sentence" in discussing Dorothy Richardson's work' (1923):

> She has invented, or if she has not invented, developed and applied to her own uses, a sentence which we might call the psychological sentence of the feminine gender. It is of a more elastic fibre than the old, capable of stretching to the extreme, of suspending the frailest particles, of enveloping the vaguest shapes.[11]

---

[10] And, whether lexical choices are empirically tested or not, one wonders, as Simpson (1993) does, how these particular words of Jespersen's cited would have been evaluated if they were identified as characteristically 'male' usage (Paul Simpson, *Language, Ideology and Point of View* (Routledge, London, 1993), p. 162).
[11] From a review of *Revolving Lights* (*TLS* 19.5.23), reprinted in Cameron, ed., op. cit., (1990), pp. 72–3.

Jeffries herself suggests that appositional structures, a characteristic feature of contemporary feminist poetry, might be regarded as an illustration of this 'elastic fibre'. Both she and Louise Sylvester also quote from the famous passage in A Room of One's Own (1929), where, after lamenting the lack of a 'common sentence' ready for the female novelist to use, Woolf describes the style she finds typical of nineteenth-century writers like Thackeray, Balzac and Dickens and then states:

> That is a man's sentence; behind it one can see Johnson, Gibbon and the rest. It was a sentence that was unsuited for a woman's use . . .'[12]

Irritatingly, Woolf does not specify the kind of sentence that was suited for a woman's use; but, as Sylvester indicates, it is likely to be non-periodic. This could either mean 'loose' in the rhetorical sense of favouring right-branching structures (main clause plus subordinate clause(s)) as against the left-branching structures of the periodic sentence (the main clause delayed until the end: harder to process); or 'loose' in the sense of favouring co-ordination rather than subordination, with implicit as well as explicit co-ordination. Certainly, appositional structures could be put in this latter category.

There are some significant (and rather complex) caveats to make about Woolf's statements. Her own prose style as the 1920s progressed, like the work of Richardson whom she admires, was attempting to capture the relatively 'new' domain in the novel of internal mental perspective and focalization, and of trying to represent, moreover, the new domain of female subjectivity, the 'flow' of a woman character's thoughts, her idiosyncratic mind-set and her feelings, her 'world-view'. For this a looser, non-periodic style would be more appropriate, but to some extent applies whether a character is male or female. As Woolf says in her review of 1923 cited above, 'Miss Richardson has fashioned her sentence consciously, in order that it may descend to the depths and investigate the crannies of Miriam Henderson's consciousness'. Indeed, the phrase 'stream-of-consciousness' was first applied to Richardson's work, by May Sinclair in The Egoist in 1918. But Woolf also vaguely states: 'Other writers of the opposite sex have used sentences of this description and stretched them to the

---

[12] Virginia Woolf, A Room of One's Own (1929); this edition Grafton Books, London, 1989, p. 73.

extreme.' One traditional literary way of representing thought processes was through the indirect symbolization of rambling speech: so
Hardy suggests (1990) that both Woolf and Richardson were influenced by Shakespeare and Dickens' talkative women, the very writers
whom Jespersen may have had in mind.[13] Thus, as Hardy says, we
have a woman's imitation of a man's imitation of a woman's talkativeness. But Woolf may also have had James Joyce in mind, whose
*Ulysses* had been published in 1922. He certainly pushed language to
an 'extreme', and his extended representation of the thoughts of
Molly Bloom has long been regarded by critics (some female) as a
stylistic tour de force. The possible influence of male writers on Woolf
and Richardson certainly complicates the issue of gender differences
in writing, at least if 'gender' is simply equated with 'sex': gender style
as a construct or a position I shall return to below. In Joyce's case,
however, there is the distinct possibility that his own work was influenced by Richardson's (her *Pointed Roofs*, the first part of *Pilgrimage*,
had appeared in 1915), although this was never openly acknowledged.
The other main caveat concerns Woolf's notion (1929) that the
sentences inherited from Johnson and Gibbon, etc. were unsuited to
women's use, and the implication that they were better off with a
non-periodic style. In one light, her comments are not far removed
from Jespersen's, and what might lie behind both sets of generalizations is the social and cultural fact, as Hardy notes (1990), that
generations of intelligent women had been deprived of education, and
particularly a classical education, which would have schooled them in
rhetorical stylistic and structural techniques and an impersonal, authoritative mode of writing. Much feminist criticism has now traced the
pattern of women's literacy and education, and the implications of the
lack of both for their access to the 'high' genres of poetry, epic and
drama, as well as the 'public' spheres of law, government, religion,
etc., and the corresponding discourses of 'power'. A sense of 'exile', of
'alienation' from such domains comes over indeed in *A Room of One's
Own*, and generic questions and explorations have become a fruitful
area of study: women's traditional access to the 'marginalized' or
'private' writing of diaries and letters, for example.

Generic features and conventions themselves, it has to be said,
present a problem for stylistic research into gender differences (see

---

[13] Barbara Hardy, 'The Talkative Woman', in Sally Minogue, ed., *Problems
for Feminist Criticism* (Routledge, London, 1990), pp. 20 and 33.

below); but there are still interesting questions to ponder about the traditional demarcation of genres. So Louise Sylvester's tentative conclusions in this volume about the styles of Walter de la Mare and Eleanor Farjeon in the genre of 'fairy tales', could be seen to highlight both the problem of the deterministic power of conventions, and the possibility that de la Mare is 'appropriating' a genre that is traditionally associated with the private and domestic sphere of a female 'teller'. Alienation has become an important general issue in feminist criticism, both literary and linguistic. Feminist linguists following Spender (1980) have suggested that the 'common language' (Adrienne Rich) between men and women has been traditionally appropriated by men, and women subordinated or even excluded altogether, silenced.[14]

The 'silent woman', as the work of Coates and Cameron reveals, is an enduring image rendered desirable to centuries of men, who have believed that not only are women talkative, but talk too much, and like children, should be seen and not heard. The image finds persistent embodiment in drama, where the speaking voice and speech acts are foregrounded: Jonson's *Epicoene, or The Silent Woman,* for instance; and, very viciously, in Shakespeare's *Titus Andronicus,* with the maiming of Lavinia. This physical, literal, 'taking the words out of one's mouth', is, as Anne Varty reveals in this volume, the preoccupation of Timberlake Wertenbaker's play *The Love of the Nightingale* (1988), itself based on the classical myth where Philomele is similarly maimed. Silence is thus a symbol of oppression,of powerlessness, as Varty further demonstrates.[15]

The so-called 'common language' described above, therefore, largely reflect the preoccupations, the perceptions, the world-view and ideological perspective of men. As Lesley Jeffries' chapter reveals the poetry of Adrienne Rich and others tries to find a voice, a new language for the embodiment of female experience, within a genre that has traditionally been the 'high' province of the male voice. The search for a new or authentic language is also the concern of many contemporary women novelists, such as Keri Hulme and Margaret Attwood, as Marion Lomax demonstrates in her chapter.

As Lomax also indicates, the search for a women's liberating

---

14 Dale Spender, *Man Made Language* (Routledge, London, 1980).
15 See also Catherine Belsey's chapter, 'Silence and Speech' in her *The Subject of Tragedy* (Methuen, London, 1985). Silence, it has to be said, can be in some contexts a symbol of defiance, of subversion.

language and style has been the long-time concern of French feminists in particular, who have popularized the term *écriture féminine*.
Again, Woolf's own voice, 'The book has somehow to be adapted to
the body' (A *Room of One's Own*, p. 74) appears to be echoed in
French feminist theory, in sentiments like Irigaray (1977), who states:
'The question of language is closely allied to that of feminine sexuality
. . . I raise the question of . . . a language that would be adequate for
the body, sex and the imagination . . . of the woman . . .'[16] Only in
such a language, and a language which is rhythmic, pluralistic, in-
determinate, flowing and ecstatic, can women's experience(s), according to Irigerary, Kristeva and Cixous, be adequately expressed, and
apparently 'fixed' meanings be unsettled and disrupted.

Clearly, there are several problems with this kind of stylistic charac-
terization. Granted that it might be difficult for women to find a
stylistic 'space' that is not occupied by men, what emerges is a kind of
definition that is still marked by the presence of men, in that they
provide the 'norm' for the resulting anti-norm. If men's style is 'rational', women's must therefore be 'emotional', even 'irrational'; if
'logical', then women's must be 'illogical', and so on. And while it
may be praiseworthy to turn negative attributions into positive (a
trend also followed in feminist sociolinguistics) the resulting discourse
can still give the impression of reinforcing all the stereotypical images
of women's discourse and style that have been referred to earlier.

More broadly, there has been a turning away in French
(-influenced) criticism, following the direction of post-modernism,
from the assumption that stylistic differences reflect sexual or biological, rather than 'gender' differences. As Easthope and McGowan put
it (1992), identity becomes an effect rather than simply an origin of
linguistic practice.[17] And so, as the work of Kristeva reveals, *l'écriture
féminine* can be regarded as a discourse construct open to both men
and women; and related earlier styles, e.g. that of modernism and
symbolist poetry (by male writers) appropriated to this mode, as well
as the styles of Derrida and Lacan. One problem is that until social
perspectives change, and the balance of 'power' shifts (see below),
*écriture féminine* will always be seen to lack the voice of authority. And
one irony, of course, is that many women writers can be seen to have

---

[16] Luce Irigaray, 'Women's Exile', *Ideology and Consciousness*, 1 (1977),
quoted Debbie Cameron, op. cit. (1985), p. 128.
[17] Antony Easthope and Kate McGowan, eds., A *Critical and Cultural
Theory Reader* (Open University Press, Buckingham, 1992), p. 68.

only succeeded traditionally in their careers by 'code-switching', adopting *l'écriture masculine*, the dominant literary mode, even assuming male writing 'identities'. And even at the present moment, it has to be said that for many women still, social and cultural forces strongly influence gender positions, in terms of opposition and difference, in spoken and written discourses.

Interestingly, the study by sociolinguists and discourse analysts of one social force, that of 'power', is proving to have significant consequences for the discussion of gender differences, to the extent also, however, that this particular perspective is now being cross-cut by others, such as education, race and class. Traditionally denied positions of high status and the corresponding 'high' styles of prestige as indicated earlier, many women in conversational interaction between the sexes reveal linguistic features of 'subordination': more hesitations, pauses and hedges; with particular functions of tag-questions and modal verbs, for example. As Varty reveals in her chapter, silence plays a part here: women listening to men talking, not speaking out of turn, or interrupting: generally, being very accommodating. Accommodation can also take the form of marked politeness and of the continual need to save the addressee's 'face'.

Educated women, of course, like the contributors to this volume, may not see themselves as doing what has been termed the 'shitwork' of mixed-sex conversation, and have undoubtedly appropriated, along with the complex or periodic sentence, the discourse strategies of power for themselves. But the power struggle is not just a matter of prestige and/or education: any group of people, of either sex will reveal differences of status, according to age, occupation, degree of friendship, culture and situation, etc. Far too many generalizations are made on the basis of sexual differences only, and on the basis of restricted evidence: e.g. that women are more 'co-operative' in their conversational style with each other, and that men are more 'competitive'.

The fact, nonetheless, that women talking to each other has become the subject of recent research in feminist sociolinguistics (somewhat unfortunately labelled 'gossip')[18] has interesting implications for feminist stylistics, since it could be fruitfully interwoven with the exploration in literary criticism since the 1980s of the tradition of

---

[18] See Deborah Jones, 'Gossip: notes on women's oral culture', in C. Kramarae, ed., *The Voices and Words of Women and Men* (Pergamon Press, Oxford, 1980).

'romantic friendship' between women.[19] In this volume, Clara Calvo's analysis of the strategies of the conversational exchanges and shifts in the dynamics of intimacy between Rosalind and Celia in *As You Like It* suggests useful possibilities for further research, even within the context of Shakespeare's own work. In this play, romantic friendship precedes heterosexual love and is so foregrounded, even though Celia's loving influence must be superseded by Orlando's at the close.

Of course, Shakespeare's women were portrayed by male actors, and often, like Rosalind, assumed male 'disguise'; but even if we were not convinced that Celia and Rosalind's discourses were plausibly 'feminine', they do still illustrate the point made above that certain strategies and styles of speech may well indeed be open to both sexes according to various social and contextual factors. And of course, we are also confronted here with the general issue of the representation of women in male-authored fiction referred to at the beginning of this introduction, an aspect of 'feminist critique'.

The two essays which conclude this volume by Shan Wareing and Sara Mills highlight the issue of images of women in fiction and popular culture, and the problems raised and conclusions to be reached when texts or discourses are written, composed or performed by women. Despite thirty years of feminist awareness and consciousness raising, social stereotypes still abound in literature, which has the power to create myths as well as to represent them. (It has to be said, of course, that some social practices outside literature are still very conservative and unfavourable to many women.) Both essays reveal, through the application of Halliday's systemic grammar to the analysis of particular texts, the strong gender socialization in our society, and the striking binary contrast of activity (male) and passivity (female) that permeates, for example, the facts and fictions of sex and love.

However, as Mills implies, it is one thing to present the problem, another to explain it. The myths or stereotypes of romance may well be in part borrowed from male-authored and male-perspectived popular fiction, since they are strikingly similar (the passive lover, virgin bride, perfect wife and mother, etc.); but they are also myths we all live by, to the extent that they are part of our 'reality' and vocabulary. So too the clichés of pop songs pass into our lives, and the clichés of everyday life pass into our pop songs. It is no wonder, then, that

[19] See, for example, Lillian Faderman, *Surpassing the Love of Men; Romantic Friendship and Love between Women from the Renaissance to the Present* (Morrow, New York, 1981).

popular women's romances have attracted plentiful, yet diverse critical views: for some readers, for instance, the 'passive' woman is a
fantasy figure, far removed from the present-day reality, like the
'happy ever after' conclusion where marriage and children are the
desirable (and only) goal. But for others this conclusion is still socially
valid, and they collude in a belief-system where 'Mr Right' exists, or
where the dominance of the male is taken for granted or devoutly
wished for. Yet, as Mills concludes, analysts may well fail to appreciate
the contradictions at the heart of any apparently simple ideology. So,
too ready to assume an 'active' (positive)/ 'passive' (negative) dichotomy, we may not appreciate that the popularity of romance fiction
for many women is precisely because the (passive) female has the
power to attract and to 'tame' the (active) wild male, to 'convert' him
to love, to 'capture' him: other metaphors associated with the ideology of romance.

In the genre of romance, and pulp-fiction generally, there is much
further exploration needed, following Wareing, of the similarities and
differences in ideologies and lexical and semantic fields between
novels and stories written for men and those for women readers.[20] In
this area, as in other areas, the contributions to this volume stimulate
ideas for further research. With close attention paid to a variety of
texts, sub-genres and sub-cultures, of different historical periods, feminist linguistics and stylistics in literary criticism of the future can lead
the way to a deconstruction and reassessment of the monolithic con-
cepts of 'feminine', and also, 'masculine' styles. And, using sociolinguistic insights, they can lead the way also to a fresh consideration of
the whole space occupied by all writers regardless of their sex. Only
then will writers, and speakers, feel truly comfortable with the idea of
a 'common language', advocated nearly seventy years ago by Woolf
again, in A Room of One's Own.[21]

[20] A start has been made in Walter Nash, Language in Popular Fiction (Longman, London, 1990).
[21] I should like to thank the British Academy/ Leverhulme Trust for their
support during the preparation of this Introduction by the award of a Senior
Research Fellowship until October 1993.

# Gendered Writing and
# the Writer's Stylistic Identity

## MARION LOMAX

THE BONE PEOPLE was Keri Hulme's first novel and, although it won
the 1985 Booker McConnell Prize, early responses were not favour-
able. In her preface to its first edition (subtitled, 'standards in a
non-standard book'), Hulme lists some of the reasons publishers gave
to explain its initial rejection: one of these was that it was 'too
*different* when compared with the normal shape of novel' (Hulme,
1983).[1] In writing her book, Hulme challenged what constituted the
'normal shape', not just for a novel, but also for a word and for a
person. Later in her preface, she wrote:

> I think the *shape* of words brings a response from the reader – a tiny,
> subconscious, unacknowledged but definite response. "OK" studs a
> sentence. "Okay" is a more mellow flowing word when read si-
> lently. "Bluegreen" is a meld, conveying a colour neither blue nor
> green but both: "blue-green" is a two-colour mix.

Here is an attempt to convey mood, tone, or semantic precision
through visual shape: it is only one of many elements which create
Hulme's individual writing style.

Not all writers of fiction and poetry are also critics and theorists,
but every writer has his or her own particular writing practice, and
this may be accidentally or purposefully allied to the literary and
linguistic theories currently dominating the academic world, although
there may also be individual, and important deviations. The degree to
which the ideas of writers and feminist theorists coincide in relation
to the writing process and the individuality of the writer's style will be
explored in a selection of contemporary women's writings. I will also
investigate the case for gendered writing and the potential this phenomenon has for the writer pursuing individual expression.

Some women writers continue to express themselves in traditional,

---

[1] Keri Hulme, *The Bone People* (Spiral, New Zealand, 1983).

patriarchal ways, but they are fewer in number than they were almost
twenty years ago when Hélène Cixous claimed:

> Most women are like this: they do someone else's – man's – writing,
> and in their innocence sustain it and give it voice, and end up
> producing writing that's in effect masculine. Great care must be
> taken in working on feminine writing not to get trapped by names:
> to be signed with a woman's name doesn't necessarily make a piece
> of writing feminine. It could quite well be masculine writing, and
> conversely, the fact that a piece of writing is signed with a man's
> name does not in itself exclude femininity. It's rare, but you can
> sometimes find femininity in writings signed by men: it does hap-
> pen. (Cixous, 1976).[2]

Here, Cixous uses the terms, 'feminine' and 'masculine' to refer to
writing styles which other critics, side-stepping her focus on gender,
might prefer to call 'avant-garde' and 'traditional'. We may no longer
be 'trapped by names' in the way Cixous originally suggested, but the
appropriation of the same terms by different branches of feminist
theory has led to new confusions. It is important to distinguish between a 'patriarchal' style, whose characteristics are associated with
male supremacy and the denial of free feminine expression, and a
'masculine' style which may not be patriarchal. Then there have been
a number of male writers who, far from being in tune with what Julia
Penelope (Stanley) and Susan J. Wolfe call 'patriarchal expressive
modes' – those which reflect:

> an epistemology that perceives the world in terms of categories,
> dichotomies, roles, stasis, and causation

have found themselves veering towards modes of expression which

> reflect an epistemology that perceives the world in terms of ambi-
> guities, pluralities, processes, continuities, and complex relation-
> ships (Thorne, Kramarae, and Henley, 1983)[3]

---

[2] Hélène Cixous, 'Castration or decapitation?', *Signs*, 7, 1 (1976), (41–55)
p. 52.
[3] Julia Penelope (Stanley) and Susan J. Wolfe, 'Consciousness as style: style
as aesthetic', in Barrie Thorne, Cheris Kramarae, and Nancy Henley, eds.,
*Language, Gender and Society* (Newbury House Publishers, Rowley, Massa-
chusetts, 1983), (125–139) p. 126.

– what Julia Penelope and Susan Wolfe call 'female' and French feminists, such as Cixous, might refer to as 'feminine'.

Basic assumptions about identity, language, and meaning must be questioned when the gender of the writing style appears not to match the sex of the writer. It is important not to be led astray by labels: the adoption of a so-called 'feminine' mode of writing does not necessarily mean that the text is, therefore, 'feminist' in other respects: the work of Laurence Sterne in *Tristram Shandy*, or that of James Joyce in *Ulysses*, may combine a so-called 'feminine' style with patriarchal content.

But what of the relationship between 'feminine' and 'masculine' styles? The latter, according to Peter Schwenger's essay, 'The Masculine Mode' (Showalter, 1989),[4] is concerned with writing the male body into the text as a counterpart to the way Annie Leclerc, Hélène Cixous, Luce Irigaray, and others focus on woman's sexuality as a positive force in *her* use of language. Cixous directs woman to

Write yourself. Your body must be heard. Only then will the immense resources of the unconscious spring forth (Cixous, 1975)[5]

while in *This sex which is not one* Irigaray puns on the Freudian notion that woman is defined by her lack of sex [phallus] to assert a positive plurality in female sexuality which is reflected in her linguistic discourse:

in which "she" goes off in all directions and in which "he" is unable to discern the coherence of any meaning. Contradictory words seem a little crazy to the logic of reason, and inaudible for him who listens with ready-made grids, a code prepared in advance.

(Irigaray, 1977)[6]

Perhaps we should, like Cixous, ultimately move towards a bisexuality which is not 'the classic conception of bisexuality' (with its tendency

4 Peter Schwenger, 'The Masculine Mode' in Elaine Showalter, ed., *Speaking of Gender* (Routledge, New York and London, 1989), pp. 101–112.
5 Hélène Cixous, 'The Laugh of the Medusa' (1975) in Elaine Marks and Isabelle de Courtivron, eds., *New French Feminisms* (Harvester, Brighton, 1981), (245–64) p. 250.
6 Luce Irigaray, 'Ce sexe qui n'en est pas un' (1977), translated by Claudia Reeder in Elaine Marks and Isabelle de Courtivron, eds., *New French Feminisms* (Harvester, Brighton, 1981), (99–106) p. 103.

to merge sexual differences and 'annul' them) but is what she terms 'the other bisexuality' which 'stirs . . . up' differences, 'pursues them, increases their number' (Cixous, 1975).[7] According to Cixous, this kind of bisexual writing can be practiced by both men and women, but in her view it is more likely to be found in women's texts, men being more often 'poised to keep glorious phallic monosexuality in view'.[8] This theory allows sexual identities to be expressed in positive ways by both sexes:

> The 'other bisexual' writing is concerned with: each one's location in self . . . of the presence – variously manifest and insistent according to each person, male or female – of both sexes, nonexclusion either of the difference or of one sex, and, from this "self-permission," multiplication of the effects of the inscription of desire, over all parts of my body and the other body.
>
> (Cixous, 1975)[9]

While some men may choose to write their bodies in a 'masculine' sense, which does not deny women the right to equivalent expression, Antonin Artaud, Samuel Beckett, James Joyce, and Stephane Mallarmé are all cited by Julia Kristeva in relation to texts which show evidence of what she calls the 'semiotic chora' (Kristeva, 1974),[10] which has its roots in the pre-verbal rhythmic pulsions or drives experienced by the unborn child of either sex. Here, the association with the feminine arises because of the significant role played by the mother's body: Kristeva is not suggesting that it signifies a distinctly female kind of writing, but that an identification with the maternal is necessary in any act of creation.

Concerned with silence as well as with sound, the semiotic is a disruptive dimension in its focus on absence and meaninglessness and, being pre-verbal, Kristeva sets it against Jacques Lacan's 'symbolic order', associated with patriarchy and the child's move into the world of male-dominated language once it is born. The majority of Kristeva's examples associated with the semiotic are, ironically, by male writers

---

7  Hélène Cixous (1975), op. cit., p. 254.
8  Ibid.
9  Ibid.
10 Julia Kristeva, *La Révolution du langue poétique* (Seuil, Paris, 1974). Translated as *Revolution in Poetic Language* by Margaret Waller, introduction by Léon S. Roudiez (Columbia University Press, New York, 1984). See Chapters 2 and 12 in particular.

who are revolutionary in their disruption of the symbolic. In such writing, she discerns rhythms of the body and the unconscious working as an underlying drive or play of forces within the language. These can create a musicality in the writing and may also be at the root of contradictions and ambiguities which work against traditional expectations of meaning.

It is possible to see how Kristeva's theory could be a liberating influence on any writer who resists the limitations of language which, until recently, has evolved largely to suit the requirements of particular kinds of men; and it is easy to draw an analogy between writers, particularly women writers, and young children who are forced to function in the symbolic order, struggling to use language which often seems inadequate to express the full complexity of an experience. Angela Carter articulated the problem in relation to women when she said:

> . . . this, of course, is why it is so enormously important for women to write fiction *as* women – it is part of the slow process of decolonising our language and our basic habits of thought . . . It has nothing at all to do with being a 'legislator of mankind' or anything like that; it is to do with the creation of a means of expression for an infinitely greater variety of experience than has been possible heretofore, to say things for which no language previously existed.
> (Wandor, 1983)[11]

Kristeva's semiotic might help to provide what Angela Carter sought, but how would this work? Part of the problem for women, and writing women in particular, is that, as Maggie Humm puts it, 'The linguistic means by which men colonise women is that they devalue sensuality in favour of symbolism.' (Humm, 1986)[12] By remaining in touch with the sensual qualities of the semiotic this could be overcome to some degree. Although many writers obviously lose contact with it as children and are too perfectly assimilated into the symbolic order, the semiotic may, according to Kristeva, survive in a semi-buried state; and finding a 'genotext' (which includes 'semiotic processes but also the advent of the symbolic'[13]) within a text requires:

11 Angela Carter, 'Notes from the Front Line', in Michelene Wandor, ed., *On Gender and Writing* (Pandora, London, 1983), (69–77) p. 75.
12 Maggie Humm, *Feminist Criticism* (Harvester, Brighton, 1986), p. 44.
13 Toril Moi, ed., *The Kristeva Reader* (Blackwell, Oxford, 1986), p. 120.

pointing out the transfers of drive energy that can be detected in phonematic devices (such as the accumulation and repetition of phonemes or rhyme) and melodic devices (such as intonation or rhythm) . . . The genotext is . . . a *process*, which tends to articulate structures that are ephemeral (unstable, threatened by drive charges . . .) and non-signifying . . .' (Kristeva, 1974)[14]

The 'literary texts of the avant-garde' in which she finds genotexts are mainly by men, and because these also contain the 'advent of the symbolic', the semiotic drives are not solely in control. In the work of some women writers, such as Sylvia Plath, Kristeva links unstemmed semiotic forces with a move towards 'psychosis or suicide' (Kristeva, 1974).[15] In such cases the semiotic is not seen as a means to achieve positive stylistic identity and fulfilment in expression, but as a desperate form of retreat which leads the woman writer towards extinction in her bid to free herself from the traps of language and meaning. A male writer could also take this route, as in the case of certain American poets, whose response to their enforced involvement in the Vietnam War was to turn against the language of the culture which sent them and resort to expressing themselves mainly through sounds and rhythms.[16]

The need for a consensus of basic communication indicates that to retain no links with the symbolic would be unwise and would lead to too personal a response which could bypass the referential code altogether and might be taken to signify madness. Whatever the nature of language or the symbolic (and it is not always accepted that this *is* patriarchal),[17] it is what we have, and disruption rather than desertion is a compromise many writers prefer.

The nature of poetry should make it an ideal medium in which the semiotic can surface in a positive way. Much of the poetry of the Northern Irish poet, Medbh McGuckian, for example, would seem to be based on elements which Kristeva identifies. Yet, when a writer appears to be in line with a 'theory', it is easy (and would be unwise)

---

14 Op. cit., pp. 120–21.

15 Ibid., p. 158.

16 I refer you to the unpublished work of Tim Woods, Department of English, University of Aberystwyth.

17 Sandra M. Gilbert and Susan Gubar question this in 'Sexual Linguistics: Gender, Language, Sexuality', in *The Feminist Reader: Essays in Gender and the Politics of Literary Criticism*, ed. Catherine Belsey and Jane Moore (Methuen, London, 1989), pp. 81–99.

to forget that the writer's own, individual needs came first. Attempting to summarize McGuckian's work, Blake Morrison writes:

> Her poetry is rhapsodic in its rhythms and often surrealistic in its imagery – describing what it means is never easy.
>
> (Morrison, 1993)[18]

Perhaps this is because the non-signifying processes have become part of the meaning.

McGuckian strives to articulate ideas which resist definition in the usual way – depths and nuances of emotion, spirituality – so her style is likely to stem directly from the need to find a powerful means of expression in specific instances and would not, then, spring from a conscious effort on her part to adopt a particular writing mode. It is unsatisfactory to take part of a work out of context, but the fourth stanza of her poem, 'Field Heart', illustrates possible links with Kristeva's semiotic:

> Nothing was to be seen through the closed lids
> of your eventful dreaming,
> the closed avenue of your new senses
> beginning as absolute strangers
> their ready-to-be-reaped, matured homecoming.[19]

The main concern of the poem seems to be to celebrate and evoke a sense of the 'loosened soul' addressed in the final stanza, within a context of 'union' – both with the speaker and 'all the Irelands'. Her task involves articulating an absence through an imagined, but insubstantial presence.

In the stanza quoted, there are ambiguities and pluralities expressed in the juxtaposition of 'closed' and 'eventful' and in the playful oppositions of 'closed avenue', 'new senses/ beginning', and 'ready-to-be-reaped, matured homecoming'. The poem creates, simultaneously, an impression of death in life and life in death – of old sensory faculties which reacted to the earthly existence, being transformed into 'new senses' ('absolute strangers'), for the non-earthly stages of the journey towards a 'homecoming' which, despite their newness, is 'ready-to-be-

---

18 Blake Morrison, 'Contemporary Poets', in *The Independent on Sunday*, 11 April 1993, p. 34.
19 Medbh McGuckian, 'Field Heart', in *The Independent on Sunday*, 11 April 1993, p. 34.

reaped, matured'. The prevalence of multi-syllabic words with their final, unstressed syllables at the ends of lines (not strictly speaking, so-called 'feminine rhymes', but working in the same way) produces a fluid rhythm which delays closure.

In the case of Irish writers working in English, and others who have a complex linguistic heritage, what Kristeva calls traces of the semiotic may also be associated with features of a buried mother tongue. Even when writers no longer speak it, it may still influence rhythms and basic attitudes to language. Irish, for example, seems closer to the semiotic than the symbolic in the way it often expresses meaning obliquely rather than directly. An awareness of multiplicity in language is not the sole preserve of women writers, as Kristeva has shown. Bilingual writers of both sexes have also entered the arena. Nicole Ward Jouve explains her own case:

So in some ways French began to function for me as a language of 'origins'. As a 'maternal' language, in opposition to English which I must have cast in the role of the 'patriarchal', a 'symbolic', a law-giving language. (Monteith, 1986)[20]

Her collection of short stories, Le spectre du gris (Shades of Grey), begins with a young French mother expressing her alienation in a regimented English hospital. The English title, 'Forceps Birth' (in the French edition it is 'Qu'elles'), refers more to the mother's forced delivery into the cold, artificially lit, white ward of a foreign language than it does to the physical birth of her child.

She clings to soft, 'babble-like', 'poetic' French reminiscences as a defence against this. Revealingly, those bits proved untranslatable and were left out of the English edition. (Monteith, 1986)[21]

The subject, who has a crisis of identity after the birth of her daughter in more ways than one, is known simply as 'E.', something less than 'Elle', certainly a French identity rather than her English name by

---

[20] Nicole Ward Jouve, ' "Her legs bestrid the channel": writing in two languages', in Moira Monteith, ed., Women's Writing: a challenge to theory (Harvester, Brighton, 1986), (34–53) p. 41.
[21] Ibid.

marriage which she associates with her mother-in-law: 'When I am Mrs Wilson, je suis ma belle-mère.' (Jouve, 1977).[22] The English language alienates her from her mother tongue and the identity she has within it: 'Quand on me dit dans cette langue je cesse d'être dans la mienne. Ma. Natale.'[23] It also threatens the bond of mother and daughter: the latter has been defined by English words from birth,

Qu'elle ait ainsi commencé. Parmi ces mots, 'it's a girl', roulé langue vers palais, et non la secrète émission vers l'espace, 'c'est une fille'. Ce n'est pas ma fille, she's a girl . . .[24]

E. has been forced to enter a world where, in order to communicate, she must use a language which is alien to her. When the sounds of one language are placed in the signifying context of the other, the effect is negative: 'I' in English becomes 'aï', a cry of anguish in French: ' Le I de cette langue un cri, aï. Langue où le je se dit douleur.'[25]

In Jouve's story the maternal language (French) resists and challenges the dominant patriarchal language (English) of the subject – whether in the original French edition or her own English translation. E. cannot completely turn her back on the patriarchal language, but she refuses to allow it to erase her own sense of her identity, just as many writers prefer to disrupt and subvert the symbolic to assert their identity, rather than seek to replace it altogether.

The difficulty of trying to achieve the latter aim is highlighted by Marina Warner in her essay 'Fighting Talk' (Ricks and Michaels, 1990), where she refers to reports of an ancient women's language discovered in China in 1986 and notes that the secrecy which surrounded it, and which was necessary to protect the purity of the language, made it unavailable to other women in other cultures. She also doubts that such a language can be kept totally pure in the sense that it will inevitably be bound up with the women's 'social and historical conditions'.[26]

[22] Nicole Ward Jouve, Le Spectre du gris (Editions des femmes, Périgueux, 1977), p. 22.
[23] Ibid.
[24] Ibid., pp. 22–23.
[25] Ibid., p. 40.
[26] Marina Warner, 'Fighting Talk', in Christopher Ricks and Leonard Michaels, eds., The State of the Language (Faber, London, 1990), pp. 104–5.

The invention of a language which denies men any access would probably be objectionable to a great many writers – male and female alike. Besides, all this presupposes that the symbolic *is*, and always has been, male. Sandra M. Gilbert and Susan Gubar's persuasive essay, 'Sexual linguistics: gender, language, sexuality', challenges 'the assumption that language is man-made, and proposes that male linguistic sexism arose out of a fear precisely of female linguistic primacy' (Belsey and Moore, 1989).[27] This suggests a case of reclaiming old ground rather than setting sail to discover new. It means placing old words in new contexts, 'uncovering . . . etymologies' as Mary Daly does in *Gyn/Ecology* (Daly, 1991),[28] renaming, or creating new meanings deliberately to challenge former patriarchal usage, and tackling:

> the logical tendency of our linear-directed language that makes it impossible to think across structures of main and subordinate intention, categories of negative/positive and binary logic.
>
> (Wandor, 1983)[29]

In her futuristic novel, *The Handmaid's Tale* (Atwood, 1987),[30] Margaret Atwood draws attention to the complex relationship women (and women authors in particular) have with language; she shows how they can be manipulated through it, but also how they can use it, in their own way, to preserve themselves. The regimented, patriarchal world she portrays is woman-centred only in a purely biological sense as energies focus on the need to reproduce a select few who have brought the threat of extinction upon themselves. The text is, at all times, unstable; it works within the constraints of the protagonist's circumstances, so a tension exists between the need to use secrecy (to protect) and the desire to reveal everything (to tell her story).

We are constantly reminded that, 'This is a reconstruction. All of it is a reconstruction' (Atwood, 1987).[31] There is no straightforward linear progression, but a constant process of revision; one version of

27 Sandra M. Gilbert and Susan Gubar, op. cit., p. 225.
28 Mary Daly, *Gyn/Ecology: the metaethics of radical feminism* (Women's Press, London, 1991). First edition, 1979.
29 Wendy Mulford, 'Notes on writing: a Marxist/Feminist viewpoint', in Michelene Wandor, op. cit., (31–41) p. 34.
30 Margaret Atwood, *The Handmaid's Tale* (Virago, London, 1987).
31 Ibid., p. 144.

an event will be undermined by, 'I made that up. It didn't happen that way. Here is what happened.' (Atwood, 1987),[32] and then the final admission, 'It didn't happen that way either. I'm not sure how it happened, not exactly. All I can hope for is a reconstruction.' (Atwood, 1987).[33] Like her speaker, who rarely asserts confidently, but questions and deliberates, we learn to be wary of words until we have made them our own, to recognise that often full meaning lies somewhere beyond them or between them.

We never, for example, learn the speaker's name: she is known to us only as a 'handmaid' (her role as a bearer of children on behalf of infertile women in the ruling order), or 'Offred' (the possessive preposition plus the name of the man to whom she is assigned). Both of these terms are obviously inadequate and the reader must seek other means of identifying her. The labelling, or refusal to name personally, is partly explained as a protective measure (the character is, finally, a fugitive), but it also draws us into the text. An unknown speaker tells her story to a reader she has created through reworking the language of Descartes:

> By telling you anything at all I'm at least believing in you, I believe you're there, I believe you into being. Because I'm telling you this story I will your existence. I tell, therefore you are. (Atwood, 1987)[34]

The speaker's identity is one of storyteller, an identity woven into every part of the text – and she is given definition by the reader whom she has, herself, created:

> if it's a story, even in my head, I must be telling it to someone. You don't tell a story only to yourself. There's always someone else.
> Even when there is no one.
> A story is like a letter. Dear You, I'll say. Just you, without a name. Attaching a name attaches you to the world of fact, which is riskier . . . who knows what the chances are out there, of survival, yours? I will say you, you . . . You can mean more than one.
> You can mean thousands. (Atwood, 1987)[35]

We are to believe that what we read represents an orally told story (standing for a reality which is too painful to be confronted except as

---

32 Ibid., p. 273.          34 Ibid., p. 279.
33 Ibid., p. 275.          35 Ibid., pp. 49–50.

fiction), preserved on antiquated tape cassettes, and finally edited and set down in writing by academics in the next century: it is doubly a reconstructed work.

The fragmentary nature of the text, switching abruptly from one storyline to another ('I'm too tired to go on with this story . . . Here is a different story, a better one',[36]) is a diversionary tactic, sometimes indicating that the speaker wishes to avoid confronting painful emotions, and sometimes that the new story will help her (and the reader) make sense of her immediate situation – but the reader must jump from context to context, bridging the gaps and supplying the hidden meanings. As the speaker says, reworking a quotation from *King Lear*: 'context is all' (Atwood, 1987).[37]

In the tale, to possess free access to language and the ability to use or reject it, is an indication of power which is demonstrated in the game of Scrabble between handmaid and Commander. This is also apparent in the contrast between the static, patriarchal, quasi-biblical language imposed on the handmaids as their only authorised means of mutual communication, and the constantly shifting free play with language within the speaker's thoughts:

> I sit in the chair and think about the word *chair*. It can also mean the leader of a meeting. It can also mean a mode of execution. It is the first syllable in *charity*. It is the French word for flesh. None of these facts has any connection with the others. (Atwood, 1987)[38]

Her thoughts leap out from the same signifier, and while the anaphora and clipped sentence structures convey a sense of logical, closed statements, the final sentence sends them all spinning off separately in different directions.

Finally, it is the lack of connection which triumphs because it is precisely this which is able to convey the speaker's emotions so successfully:

> I'm sorry there is so much pain in this story. I'm sorry it's in fragments, like a body caught in crossfire or pulled apart by force. But there is nothing I can do to change it. (Atwood, 1987)[39]

The uncertainty which has accompanied us throughout ('Maybe none

---

36 Ibid., p. 138.            38 Ibid., p. 120.
37 Ibid., p. 154, p. 202.    39 Ibid., p. 279.

of this is about control. Maybe it isn't really about who can own whom, who can do what to whom and get away with it . . . Maybe it isn't . . .',[40]), and the chapters which tail off without punctuation –

> All I can hear now is the sound of my own heart, opening and closing, opening and closing, opening  (Atwood, 1987)[41]

– finally lead us to an ending which is indecisive, 'And so I step up, into the darkness within; or else the light'. Even the afterward comes to a halt with, 'Are there any questions?'.

In many ways it is possible to link Atwood's novel with a feminine style of writing which is open-ended, full of diversions, and concerned with pluralities and ambiguities, but most of her syntax is not unorthodox and, ultimately, while her content is feminist, she seems to be driven more by the challenges of storytelling than those of gender theory: perhaps this is how it should be.

In Marilynne Robinson's *Housekeeping* (Robinson, 1981),[42] the title is a good example of a word, commonly (and often dismissively) associated with female domesticity, being given new and almost sinister significance. Ruth and Lucille's grandmother exhorts them to, 'Sell the orchards . . . but keep the house. So long as you . . . own the roof above your head, you're as safe as anyone can be' (Robinson, 1981).[43] After the grandmother's death, for Ruth and her once-vagrant Aunt Sylvie, misfits in a patriarchal community which values cleanliness and order above disorganised, unconditional love, the process of 'housekeeping' becomes synonymous with the struggle to conform. The crucial decision which eventually faces them is whether to keep the house or leave it: they decide to go, so they burn it down. Ruth's inability to keep to the house, even at night, has already sealed her fate as Sylvie is deemed an unfit guardian. They are women of a new kind; paradoxically, freedom and independence can only be theirs if they accept accompanying insecurity and live without a house to keep.

The book charts, though not explicitly, the quest for an elusive mother:

---

[40] Ibid., p. 144.
[41] Ibid., p. 156.
[42] Marilynne Robinson, *Housekeeping* (Penguin, Harmondsworth, 1981).
[43] Ibid., p. 27.

If there had been snow I would have made a statue, a woman to stand along the path, among the trees. The children would have come close . . . Lot's wife was salt and barren, because she was full of loss and mourning, and looked back. But here rare flowers would gleam in her hair, and on her breast, and in her hands, and there would be children all around her, to love and marvel at her for her beauty, and to laugh at her extravegent adornments, as if they had set the flowers in her hair and thrown down all the flowers at her feet, and they would forgive her, eagerly and lavishly, for turning away, though she never asked to be forgiven. Though her hands were ice and did not touch them, she would be more than mother to them, she so calm, so still, and they such wild and orphan things.

(Robinson, 1981)[44]

This passage is based on the conditional – there is no such statue or snow. The Biblical story of Lot's wife is transformed, and Ruth's wish, which is so transparent within the rhapsodic rhythms, evokes a figure, reminiscent of her drowned mother, who will be forgiven for deserting them. Yet 'her hands were ice' suggests many things simultaneously – Ruth's inability, even in her imagination, to bring the figure to life; her willingness to settle for a remote mothering presence in the absence of a breathing reality; and her notion that nature will, ultimately, provide what she seeks.

Later, this moment is recalled when the bible is, again, evoked and Ruth adopts its language and takes its story beyond the ending and back to a new beginning:

The force behind the movement of time is a movement that will not be comforted. That is why the first event is known to have been an expulsion, and the last is hoped to be a reconciliation and return. . . .– there will be a garden where all of us as one child will sleep in our mother Eve, hooped in her ribs and staved by her spine.

(Robinson, 1981)[45]

Genesis is reworked so that Eve, the first woman who could not conform, is celebrated as the last and only mother – in a garden that was once an orchard with no house to be kept.

The rhythms of the prose are in keeping with its maternal subject, recalling Kristeva's traces of the semiotic. For Ruth, the search for a lost mother is bound up with the way Sylvie and she try to renew the

44 Ibid., p. 133.          45 Ibid.

lost bond with nature (which is never really severed, since the houses are built on a former lake which returns to flood them, and the garden constantly invades the interior). Finally, the ending resists closure and is a tour de force, creating a sense of the continuous presence out of absence and negatives. Ruth, having been long separated from her conventional sister Lucille, by her flight with Sylvie, conjures up Lucille's presence, much as she imagined the snow statue:

No one watching this woman . . . could know how her thoughts are thronged by our absence, or know how she does not watch, does not listen, does not wait, does not hope, and always for me and Sylvie. (Robinson, 1981)[46]

As in the earlier episode, Ruth's longings are expressed simultaneously with her fears that they are not possible. The novel creates a new mythology of women who find they have no choice but to rewrite, in their imaginations, the original stories which have excluded them – they must create a new beginning after the end.

In *The Bone People* the generation of a new creation story is associated with a sense of moving back in order to move forward, through the double spiral symbol of rebirth. As well as containing them (Kerewin's tower home is full of spirals; they form the kaumatua's secret design in his will; Kerewin even sings of them), Keri Hulme's novel is structured in spirals: the antidote to linear progression.

After a first reading, we return to the opening of the book with hindsight, and the words of the prologue (entitled, 'The End at the Beginning') exist in a new context. We move further inside the spiral and the characters we now know will be identified later as Simon, Joe, and Kerewin are simply 'He', 'He', and 'She'. When the focus moves from one individual's perspective to another's, the other two characters become only 'The people' or 'They' – first signifying (but not specifically naming) Joe and Kerewin, then Kerewin and Simon, finally Joe and Simon (Hulme, 1986).[47] The last section of the prologue provides the rationale behind Hulme's naming process, where a word like 'people', usually taken to be a general descriptor, is substituted for three specific names and becomes a type of name in itself:

46 Ibid.
47 Keri Hulme, *The Bone People* (Picador, London, 1986), p. 3.

They were nothing more than people, by themselves. Even paired, any pairing, they would have been nothing more than people by themselves. But all together, they have become the heart and muscles and mind of something perilous and new, something strange and growing and great. Together, all together, they are the instruments of change. (Hulme, 1986)[48]

Individual identity depends on corporate identity – and this does not entail familiar binary pairings, but is a ternary structure, a new trinity. The number three and its combinations are everywhere apparent. When Joe is imprisoned for beating the child, Simon, the sentence is three months. Kerewin leaves her tower wondering 'if she would still be alive three months from now', and takes three significant books with her. Joe Gillayley, like Christ, is thirty-three years old at the time of his most severe trials (as is the speaker in *The Handmaid's Tale*). Three, as Mary Daly demonstrates, in her discussion of the triple goddesses of early mythology (Daly, 1991),[49] is an important number in a huge range of religions, not just Christianity.

As a whole, the novel achieves what feminist theories often advocate: the breakdown of binary modes of thought. Hulme rejects the usual sexual pairings – both heterosexual and homosexual: the union she advocates is between three people, as depicted in the tricephalos which Kerewin sculpts – their three faces on one head. Hulme also destroys the notion that people automatically fall clearly into one of two sex categories and creates a third possibility. Kerewin sees herself as 'neuter' and she invents a 'neuter personal pronoun' for both herself and the character (neither male nor female) who appears in her illness to minister to her, like her own, personal, neuter guardian – 've/ver/vis, I am not his, vis/ve/ver, nor am I for her, ver/vis/ve, a pronoun for me' (Hulme, 1986).[50] Nor does Simon, with his long blond hair and counter-tenor singing, fit easily into the usual categories: 'Is it a boy or a girl?', asks the barman (Hulme, 1986).[51]

New phenomena need new names and Hulme's naming process takes the form of riddles (as in 've/ver/vis') or puns. In the prologue there appears to be no name for the characters' new identity as a corporate body signifying change, but to find this we need to move to the closing pages where Simon is contemplating:

---

48 Ibid., p. 4.
49 Mary Daly, op. cit., pp. 75–79.

50 Keri Hulme, op. cit., p. 426.
51 Ibid., p. 244.

He doesn't know the words for what they are. Not family, not whanau . . . maybe there aren't words for us yet? (E nga iwi o nga iwi, whispers Joe) (Hulme, 1986)[52]

To find the meaning of the Maori words we turn to the final page:

. . . this is a pun. It means, O the bones of the people (where 'bones' stands for ancestors or relations), or, O the people of the bones (i.e. the beginning people, the people who make another people)

Now, we move from the last page to the first, where the name we seek is the title, *The Bone People*: we have moved in a spiral.

*The Bone People* can be considered a 'meld' (to use Hulme's word from her preface) of many religions, languages, cultures, texts and symbolisms. It is eclectic and multiple. Like 'bluegreen' which is not 'a two-colour mix' but conveys 'a colour neither blue nor green but both', the meld of the book as a whole suggests that its many elements are not mixed (so that individual features are lost), but are simultaneously expressed as a new, corporate creation. This will also be the nature of 'the bone people', the 'people who make another people' – for, however this is to come about, it will not be through straightforward biological mixing. There are no blood ties between Kerewin, Joe, and Simon – yet, the novel suggests, new people will be 'born' out of the pain and love found in their unusual relationship. Apart from the linear process of biological creation, in which ancestors breed descendants (recalling the Maori pun where 'bones' stand for ancestors) – there is also another, simultaneous possibility (as the pun implies), that people like Kerewin, Joe, and Simon can be born out of their former selves, recreated as a corporate being, a new people. The phoenix is, after all, another prevalent image in the book: the tricephalos is fired in a 'pyre' while Kerewin muses, 'Who knows what will rise if it hatch?'(Hulme, 1986).[53]

*The Bone People* is full of bodies and structures which are broken and then reassembled in new ways. Kerewin's tower, which has 'a skeleton, wooden ribs and girdle, skin of stone' (Hulme, 1986),[54] is first associated only with herself, but later comes to stand for all three: it is dismantled at the time when Joe, Kerewin, and Simon are separated. Towards Christmas, the birth-time set for their reunion, Kerewin

52 Ibid., p. 395.                    54 Ibid., p. 7.
53 Ibid., p. 320

completes the building of the Maori hall and brings together the lost bones of the shipwreck from which Simon was rescued. A new, 'round shell house' is built to 'hold them all in its spiralling embrace' (Hulme, 1986)[55] – not just the three protagonists, but also their extended family: the bones of the three come together in one body amidst the living bones of those who are, in some cases, their ancestors.

The central pun of 'the bone people' is only one of many such riddles which serve to reveal the story to us. Clues to Simon's mysterious background are rarely given directly. When Kerewin muses, 'I'll lay a thousand on it there's a French connection somewhere' (Hulme, 1986),[56] she mentions 'Saint Clare beach, Citroen cars . . .' but later we discern a pun on the phrase, in relation to the world of drug rings, which takes us closer to the truth and the heroin smuggling and addiction in Simon's past.

Playing with words and sounds is at the heart of the unravelling. Early in the novel Joe says of Simon, 'I'm pretty sure that O'Connor was the name of the people he was with' (Hulme, 1986):[57] later, we discover that the name is 'MacDonagh' – very different on the page, but similar in sound. For Simon, words, their contexts, and what they represent, prove so painful to confront that he is unable to speak at all; making any noise himself upsets him:

'. . . The ENT bloke who examined him said there was no physical reason to prevent him from speaking. He's got all the gear needed, eh. But if he vocalises, he throws up, and violently.'
'Words?'
'No, just sounds.' (Hulme, 1986)[58]

In the three separate new versions of St John's 'In the beginning . . .' which Hulme gives us in the prologue – one for each character – Simon, at the time of the shipwreck, hears not 'the word', but 'words, different words. Help, but not help. Words. There were words' (Hulme, 1986).[59] These are words in a foreign language, presumably French, because of the association with the drug dealers, and this highlights another aspect of the novel – its attempt to make words, which may seem alien, palatable.

55 Ibid., p. 442.
56 Ibid., p. 210.
57 Ibid., p. 87.

58 Ibid., p. 86.
59 Ibid., p. 5.

In Simon's case, he eventually sidesteps language altogether and sings wordlessly but, on another level, as she states in her preface, Hulme is concerned that the reader acquires a taste for her own style:

To those used to one standard, this book may offer a taste passing strange, like the original mouthful of kina roe. Persist. Kina can become a favourite food.

Although it is not clearly allied to any particular feminist theory, her writing contains features of several. In keeping with the book's eclectic nature in all other respects, Keri Hulme breaks down binary oppositions, totally rejects a linear structure, resists closure, works through puns and pluralities, lets rhythms and sounds have free play, sets poetry alongside prose, diary entries beside dialogue, shifts in perspective against a meld of languages, includes her own invented onomatopoeia and word shapes, creates phonetic reconstructions of fragmented thoughts, and sets the language of tasting and feeding (traditionally associated with domesticity and the female) in a wider context of nurturing, healing, and consuming, which includes men as well as a non-maternal woman. Hulme's individual writing style is a product of many influences, but her attitude to the whole issue of gender plays a significant part.

# Language in Common:
## Apposition in Contemporary Poetry by Women

### LESLEY JEFFRIES

### INTRODUCTION

*Women and language*

DISCUSSIONS OF WOMEN and their relationship to language have become commonplace both inside and outside academic communities. Whilst the political importance of such widespread discussion should not be underestimated, the superficiality and simplistic nature of some aspects of the popular debate about, for example, sexism in language, often has the effect of undermining the seriousness of the subject. Many highly educated 'lay' people express outrage at such 'monstrosities' as *personhole* to replace *manhole*. Even within the academic community, some of the discussion has failed to take sufficient notice of advances in linguistic description[1] and has consequently been reductive and lacking in both linguistic and political subtlety.

Alongside the linguistic discussions of the ways in which women are disadvantaged in language there have been many literary, psychological and theoretical discussions of women's relationship to language. In all disciplines, they fall into three main categories, though these categories have no clear boundaries and indeed overlap in different ways. The categories, however, have a respectable background, being the organising principle in Deborah Cameron (ed.) *The Feminist Critique of language* (Routledge, London, 1990). The categories are: women's silence, representation of women in language and women's language itself. This chapter addresses one aspect of the third category.

Underlying all of these debates is a version of the Whorfian

---

[1] The best known example is Dale Spender's *Man Made Language* (Routledge, London, 1980) which is criticised in a review by Maria Black and Rosalind Coward in Deborah Cameron, (ed.), *A Feminist Critique of Language* (Routledge, London, 1990). They point out a number of flaws in Spender's linguistic descriptions.

hypothesis, which claims that we perceive the world through the structures set up by our language. Whilst few linguists adhere to the 'strong' version of this theory, many subscribe to a 'weaker' version, which might be paraphrased as saying that we tend to perceive the world through the structures of our language, but that we *can* perceive in other ways (in other languages, for example) and that we *can* escape the straitjacket of our own language, though we often don't.

## A new tradition?

If we accept the weak version of the Whorfian hypothesis, then the feminist who wishes to speak/write a language which more closely represents her experience must be aiming to 'escape' from the constraints of the language which currently 'trap' her.

We might ask how radical such an escape can or could be. An analogy from the visual arts might be useful to distinguish between the extremes. The advantage of using an example from a different medium is that we are avoiding the circularity which is inevitable when using language to discuss language.

The artistic tradition of the West has long been based on a version of realism which is visually determined. So, despite the different versions of realism which have informed movements of different eras (e.g. Impressionism), most of these representational techniques have made bodies in some sense look like bodies and trees look like trees. Whilst each new generation of artists criticises and rejects the previous generation, in retrospect it can be seen that they have each built upon the ideas of the past.

It is conceivable that another tradition of artistic representation could have arisen based on a different kind of realism. This might be, for example, what is known as haptic representation, which gives prominence to features in proportion to their importance. The clearest example of this would be the child's drawing which emphasises in the early stages the eyes and mouth at the expense of arms and legs.[2]

What such a tradition of art would have become by now is difficult to imagine because it is like giving someone directions by saying 'But I wouldn't have started from here'. I suggest that many writers on women's language are trying to approach the topic from just such a

---

[2] I wish to thank Trevor Edmands for the information on hapticity. If I have misunderstood the argument, the fault is mine.

point of view: a complete rejection of the patriarchal tradition of language. The practical attempts to imagine a tradition, important though they are, can only guess at the outcome and can in practical terms only use material available to the writer at the time. As Elizabeth Abel (1982)[3] says:

"A possible operation of the feminine in language" becomes, then, the revelation of its repression, through an effect of playful rehearsal, rather than a demonstrably feminine linguistic practice.

The paradox for feminists writing a new tradition is that they have to communicate with other women who are also locked into the repressive language. The question rapidly becomes a practical political one: do you aim for a genuinely radical rethink of women's language and risk losing (the comprehension of) much of your audience or do you start from where we are and gradually work toward the 'goal'? The pragmatic answer, but one that many political movements fail to recognise is that these strategies are not necessarily mutually exclusive.

## Linguistics: the 'how' of style

In reading and thinking about the issue of a women's language, I have become increasingly frustrated by the vagueness with which language is described. As an A-level English student, asked to write about the language of a text, I had no vocabulary, no tools for this job, and felt their lack keenly. As a teacher of 'Language of literature' courses, I see students who know what the effect of a piece of text is, and may even be able to say quite precisely *where* the effect is located, but are unable to say *how* it is achieved. As a reader of texts about women and their relationship with language, I want to know, for example, more precisely what Woolf *means* by 'the woman's sentence' in discussing Dorothy Richardson's work (1923):[4]

[3]  Elizabeth Abel *Writing and Sexual Difference* (Harvester, Brighton, 1982), p. 41.
[4]  From a review by Virginia Woolf of Dorothy Richardson's *Revolving Lights* (*TLS* 19 May 1923), reprinted in Deborah Cameron, *The Feminist Critique of Language* (Routledge, London, 1990), pp. 72–3. Woolf also addresses the theme of a woman's sentence in *A Room of One's Own* (1929) where she says for example: '. . . That is a man's sentence; behind it one can see Johnson,

She has invented, or, if she has not invented, developed and applied to her own uses, a sentence which we might call the psychological sentence of the feminine gender. It is of a more elastic fibre
than the old, capable of stretching to the extreme, of suspending
the frailest particles, of enveloping the vaguest shapes.

There have been some very satisfying pieces of research on the
discourse and conversational aspects of women's language, as it differs
from men's[5] which have had an effect of partially allaying this frustra-
tion. However, these studies focus on what may well be the result of a
tradition that women have had available to them through the ages:
the domestic and woman-to-woman spoken type of discourse. The
problem of what a women's tradition of literary and other written or
public language might be like is much more likely to be hypothetical,
given the intermittent nature of women's engagement with the largely
patriarchal public world.

However, women have now been writing and publishing in relatively large numbers for more than a century and the current debate
about women and language has been in the arena since at least
Virginia Woolf's time. It should therefore be possible to attempt to
define some of the areas where women (poets, for the purposes of this
study) have used the potential of the language they have 'inherited' to
suggest the features of a 'women's' language. What is not at issue here
is that much of the overtly feminist poetry written in the last twenty
years has addressed the question of women's relationship with language as its subject, without necessarily engaging in a specifically
women's linguistic practice. Jan Montefiore (1987)[6] makes a similar
distinction in relation to the poetry of Adrienne Rich:

What defines these love-poems as feminist is their subject matter
and Rich's acknowledged public identity as feminist. But injection
of new experiential content is not in itself a transformation of
poetry; though Rich, I think, would argue that it is.

Gibbon and the rest. It was a sentence that was unsuited for a woman's use.
Charlotte Brontë, with all her splendid gift for prose, stumbled and fell with
that clumsy weapon in her hands.' (Grafton Books, London, 1989), p. 73.
[5] See, for example, papers in Jennifer Coates and Deborah Cameron, eds.,
*Women in their Speech Communities* (Longman, Harlow, 1988).
[6] Jan Montefiore, *Feminism and Poetry* (Pandora, London, 1987) p. 166.

There is a shortage of linguistic analysis in the discussion of a women's tradition of language partly because twentieth century linguistics has gone so far to establish its credentials as a respectable scientific discipline that it has lost relevance for many, including feminists, who prefer to see language as a more artistic and social phenomenon. Kristeva,[7] in *The System and the Speaking Subject*, echoes this sentiment:

> the science of linguistics has no way of apprehending anything in language which belongs not with the social contract but with play, pleasure or desire (or, if it does attempt to take account of these, it is forced to infringe its epistemological purity and call itself by such names as stylistics, rhetoric, poetics.

However, the increasing prominence of previously marginal activities, such as discourse analysis and critical linguistics has helped to redeem linguistics as a vital part of any approach to language.

Some also feel that we should not lightly discard all that has come out of general linguistics or linguistic description. The years of hankering after scientific status have taught us at least the virtues of rigorous analysis, though we may want to change the way we interpret the results.[8]

The tools of linguistic description, ignoring for a moment the issue of their theoretical basis, can be used to make our appreciation of all aspects of language more subtle and our discussion of the 'how' of style more precise. Even discussions of sexist vocabulary, informed by the subtleties of lexical semantics, could possibly be redeemed!

### APPOSITION AND AMBIGUITY IN WOMEN'S POETRY:
### A CASE STUDY

*Focus on structure*

The aim of the research to be reported here was to find out *something* tangible about the language of feminist poets writing with the desire

---

[7] This extract is from Toril Moi, ed., *The Kristeva Reader* (Basil Blackwell, Oxford, 1986) p. 26.

[8] See, for example, Cameron and Coates' discussion of interpretation in sociolinguistic analysis in Chapter 2 of Jennifer Coates and Deborah Cameron, op. cit., (1988).

for a women's language in mind. The poetry I originally intended to focus upon has many linguistic features which stand out, but I was keen to look at structural rather than lexical features because of an enduring interest in syntax and its symbolic possibilities and as a reaction to the looseness of notions of a 'woman's sentence'.

One of the impressions gained by reading a great deal of feminist poetry is that there is a lack of activity, a stillness and a kind of timelessness evoked by many of the poems. These impressions are carried by techniques of writing which are far from being unique to feminist, or even women writers. However, there seems to be an unusually high concentration of such techniques in the work of some feminist poets, and this observation leads to a hypothesis that what feminists are doing in their effort to discover a woman's voice is focussing particularly on those linguistic features which reflect most closely the female experience. In terms of my earlier analogy, the tradition is not begun again from scratch, like a kind of haptic art, but is building on what is useful in the existing tradition.

The absence of punctuation in poetry is not new, although some feminist poets have seen the advantage of increasing uncertainty in the reader, sometimes leaving the reader with two or more equally possible structural interpretations. The most common type of ambiguity created in this way is where an adverbial phrase or clause occurs between two main clauses and it is unclear which main clause the adverbial belongs to:

[1]   hating you for being white
     and not me
     *in this carnival of memories*
     I name you both the laying down of power

                           (Audré Lorde[9]: *Sequelae*)

While the reader may be unsure, grammatically speaking, whether the 'carnival of memories' is the location of the 'hating' or of the 'laying down of power', as far as the poem goes it may not be important, or it may refer to both equally. This example is typical of many

9  All the poetry quoted from any one poet is from a single volume of her work. These will be noted at the first extract for each poet. Audré Lorde's poetry comes from *The Black Unicorn* (W.W. Norton and Co., New York, 1978).

where the syntax flows smoothly from one clause to the next, with few absolute boundaries between them.

The abundance of minor sentences, particularly sentences containing only a noun phrase, is another manifestation of the timelessness of some feminist poetry. Erin Mouré's poem, *South-West or Altadore*[10] opens with two noun phrases, in which there is no finite verb phrase:

[2]    Our imperfect, fleeing minds.
       The woman about to begin
       her walk thru the desert, carrying
       a small suitcase with the words
       "Eleftherias Street", folded, inside.

These noun phrases set up a static scene in which the woman represents both an individual and a larger timeless category of women who may find themselves in her situation.

A similar group of examples, which will form the subject of the rest of this chapter, is where a number of noun phrases occur in sequence, but not as separate minor sentences as in [2]. Many of these examples could be categorised as 'noun phrases in apposition' and the longer an appositive sequence continues, the more the text takes on a descriptive rather than an active demeanour:

[3]      But to ask you
         is to see only your flinch,
         and then *a sudden shadow*
         *in the corner of my eye*
         *a mote in the sky*
         *darting.*                    (Alison Fell[11]: *Love Song –*
                                       *the beginning of the end of the affair*)

Here the object of the verb 'see' is a coordinated pair of noun phrases, the second of which (i.e. 'a sudden shadow') is followed by a further co-referential noun phrase (beginning 'a mote'), which recasts the original in a different perspective. The total length of the object compared with other parts of the clause is sufficient to dominate the text at this point, giving a feeling of a lack of action or stillness.

---

[10] From Erin Mouré, *West South West* (Véhicule Press, Montreal, 1989).
[11] From Lilian Mohin, ed., *One Foot on the Mountain* (Onlywomen Press, London, 1979).

The following sections will look in more detail at the last of the structural features introduced here: the use and effects of apposition.

## Apposition

Apposition was chosen as a potentially rewarding area of investigation but it was first of all necessary to make sure that the definition of apposition was clear.

A *Grammar of Contemporary English* (1972)[12] describes in great detail the phenomenon of apposition, which is defined as having two basic features:

> Apposition resembles coordination in that typically the two or more units in apposition are constituents of the same level.

and:

> But for units to be *appositives*, *i.e.* in apposition, they must normally be identical in reference or else the reference of one must be included in the reference of the other.

These two defining features are taken as the basis of apposition for my purpose, but the detailed categorisation of different types of apposition in GCE did not seem to be appropriate for the data being studied: their examples being largely from the spoken language and referring almost exclusively to people; whereas the poetic examples to be discussed below very rarely referred to people. It is also interesting to note that Quirk et al. discuss only cases where the interpretation is very clear and often where the categorisation is based on a combination of physical features, such as the presence of definite or indefinite determiners. For example, in the section on 'Appellation', they say:

> With appellation, both appositive noun phrases are definite and the second is a proper noun:
>
> *my best friend, Peter,* was here last night        [p. 629]

Even when they are discussing ambiguity, the authors are only concerned

---

[12] Randolph Quirk, Sidney Greenbaum, Geoffrey Leech and Jan Svartvik, *A Grammar of Contemporary English* (Longman, Harlow, 1972), p. 620.

with cases where there are two or more easily distinguished readings which would normally be disambiguated in context.[13]

The next section will reveal that many poetic examples of apposition are both structurally and semantically ambiguous, but with no serious conflict of interpretation for the reader, who may be expected to accommodate more than one interpretation in any text.

Diane Blakemore, (1993)[14] provides a very convincing argument for the contextual relevance of even pre-planned reformulations, which can clearly not perform the function of self-correction as they might in the spoken language. She claims that:

> the speaker's style is a consequence of the pursuit of optimal relevance

and goes on to explain how she sees planned reformulations as being 'optimally relevant' in their context. Her work draws on that of Sperber and Wilson (1986)[15] who, she says,

> show, the fact that there is no single interpretation for a text or utterance does not mean that interpretation is not constrained at all. (p. 110)

She suggests that one of the purposes of apposition is to highlight the differences between the words or phrases which are juxtaposed, giving the reader an idea of the range of interpretations that are possible.

Blakemore argues that reformulations allow the hearer to take responsibility for deriving a range of weak implicatures and deciding which and how many of them are relevant in the context. This

---

[13] For example, a sentence such as – They called *Susan a waitress* – is triply ambiguous, the three relationships being

(1) indirect object + direct object:
   They called a waitress for Susan

(2) Direct object + object complement:
   They said Susan was a waitress

(3) Direct object + appositive:
   They called Susan who is/was a waitress                    (p. 627)

[14] Diane Blakemore 'The Relevance of Reformulations', *Language and Literature*, Vol 2.2 (1993) (101–120), p. 109.

[15] D. Sperber and D. Wilson, *Relevance* (Blackwell, Oxford, 1986).

approach to the interpretation of appositive structures will be seen to be useful in discussing the examples of women's poetry which form the data for this research.


## Noun phrase sequences

Even on an impressionistic reading, noun phrase sequences were quickly recognised as one of the striking grammatical features of feminist poetry. These surface structure strings of phrases were chosen as a linguistic feature sufficiently circumscribed for detailed analysis, but with an interesting array of semantic/pragmatic possibilities for exploration. It had been obvious from the outset that there were some examples of noun phrase sequences which were difficult to categorise neatly into either conjunction or apposition. My hypothesis was that this very syntactic looseness or vagueness may be one of the attractions of apposition for feminist writers searching for a women's language.

From the wide collection of women's poetry available to me, I chose to focus on ten poets who represented a period mainly between 1970 and the present (though some of Jenny Joseph's work originated in the 1960s). Because of the difficulty of clearly defining 'feminist' poets I decided to focus on women's poetry generally, with the possibility of looking at specifically feminist work in the light of my findings. The poets chosen, then, represent a cross-section of attitudes to feminism: although none of them is obviously hostile to the movement, the writers from Britain are less overtly feminist in their subject matter than those from the U.S. and Canada, some of whom also have a Caribbean dimension to their work. The ten poets are: Amy Clampitt, Jenny Joseph, Audré Lorde, Wendy Mulford, Ruth Padel, Marlene Nourbese Philip, Marge Piercy, Adrienne Rich, Jo Shapcott, Bronwen Wallace. The choice of poets is clearly rather subjective, being derived from my personal collection of poetry, but in the early stages of reading it was very obvious that the feature I had chosen to study was quite common.

The basis of the study reported here is neither comparative (male vs. female poetry) nor statistical (how many of each type of feature is found). The enthusiastic reader may well decide to try and find examples of the feature discussed in male poetry from the same/a different period or in women's poetry from different traditions. But I venture to suggest that apposition is more typical of women's poetry

and in some of its manifestations, of feminist poetry than of poetry by
male writers; or at least very readily exploited by feminist poets.
Though statistical proof of this assertion would be useful, it would be
quite difficult to obtain and is not the object of this chapter.

## The Study

The specimens were collected on the basis that they should show two
or more phrases which were potentially in apposition. Though any
clause elements (as well as clauses themselves) can be in appositive
relationships, I found, as expected, mainly noun phrase apposition. In
all about one hundred examples were collected, approximately ten
from each poet. After some had been discarded as being interesting
but outside the defined scope of apposition, there were 87 examples to
be examined. Each example was studied to establish a number of facts
about it: what was the syntactic role of the apposition, what was its
function in the context, how did it relate to categories of apposition
set up by studies based on other kinds of data, for example, spoken
data in Quirk et al (op. cit.) and a variety of discourse styles in
Blakemore (op. cit.)? The examples were also examined closely to see
whether they corresponded to the original definition of apposition,
i.e. were the phrases really co-referential and did they have the same
syntactic function?

In examining the examples collected, some difficulties emerged
when I attempted to categorise them according to the groupings set
out in Quirk et al. My data also seemed to divide into functional
categories, but none of these categories seemed to be structurally
defined and many examples had features of more than one category.

## Categorising apposition

METAPHOR. Whilst there are many ways in which the language can set
up metaphors[16] which will not be introduced here, there was a large
group of appositions among the data which seemed to achieve a
metaphorical effect by juxtaposing literal and metaphorical appositive

---

[16] But see, for example, my discussion of 'mini-metaphors' achieved by unusual collocation in Lesley Jeffries, *The Language of Twentieth Century Poetry*
(Macmillan, Basingstoke, 1993).

phrases. There were some examples which were on the borderlines of this group, but many of them were very clearly metaphorical in their interpretation and it is these 'central' examples which are discussed here.

In many cases, the linear arrangement of noun phrase after noun phrase in an apposition gives the metaphorical example a superficial similarity to a list of noun phrases, conjoined, but having different referents. Sometimes the danger of ambiguity or confusion is lessened by an overt punctuation marker of apposition. These markers signal to the reader that the noun phrases are intended to have the same reference and therefore have to be interpreted metaphorically.

The second and third lines of [4], for example, expand on the object pronoun, 'them', of the first line. From the context of the poem, we know that the subject is a sandbank out to sea, near a wrecked ship and repeatedly lashed by large waves. The 'them' to which the mind returns cannot be literally either a chain gang or archangels, and the juxtaposition of two such disparate nouns is also (even out-of-context) a strong hint that we are not in the literal world.

[4]   Your mind keeps turning back to look at *them* –
      *chain gang archangels that in their prismatic*
      *frenzy fall, gall and gash the daylight* . . ..
                                    (Amy Clampitt[17]: *The Outer Bar*)

In this example, as in the following one, a hyphen is used to indicate to the reader the intended co-referentiality of the nouns (or noun phrases). The interpretation of the metaphor is the next stage; here we will simply assume that the reader interprets the pronoun as referring to the waves and the metaphorical appositive noun phrase as hinting at features of the waves such as repetitive action and accompanying sound (chain gang) and in contrast their miraculous other-worldly nature (archangels).

In [5] also, the hyphen leads us to interpret the last three noun phrases as co-referential with, and therefore metaphorical versions of, 'our life'.

[17] From Amy Clampitt, *The Kingfisher* (Faber and Faber, London, 1984).

[5]    to *our life - this still unexcavated hole*
       *called civilisation, this act of translation,*
                        *this half-world.*        (Adrienne Rich[18]: V)

The reader's experience of discourse styles will perhaps also create
the impression that the three noun phrases characterising 'life' are in
the style of political rhetoric. The three-part list is well-used by many
persuasive speakers and one common feature of these lists is the use of
parallel structures which we have here in the form of the demonstra-
tive 'this' introducing each phrase. Other poetic strategies, such as
breaking the line after 'hole' and the gradually reducing length of the
three noun phrases, add to the pejorative impact of the sequence.
    Some metaphorical appositions introduce the appositive phrases
with a colon, as in [6]:

[6]    Wet is *what flows and seeps and comes again:*
       *that ocean we carry inside,*
       *a tidal pool cherished from our spawning grounds . . .*
                        (Marge Piercy[19]: *The pool that swims in us*)

Here, the complement of the verb 'be' consists of three noun
phrases, but the first one is marked out as primary, whilst the metaphorical descriptions of the water-content of human beings as ocean
and pool are clearly set out after the colon as descriptive additions.
One of the questions which will be addressed again later arises in
relation to this example. What is the status of the requirement that
appositions have the same referent, when some metaphorical versions
clearly do not?
    The three noun phrases in [6] have the same referent when consid-
ered as a set, but the metaphorical phrases do not share the same
literal referent. An ocean is rather different from a tidal pool and
although we can interpret the sequence as meaning that the poet
wishes us to see what human water content has in common with first
an ocean and then a tidal pool, the defining features of appositions
begin to seem less clear-cut.
    The next example, [7], has two noun phrases in apposition func-
tioning as a vocative before the main clause:

---

18 From Adrienne Rich, *The Dream of a Common Language* (W.W. Norton
and Co., New York, 1978).
19 From Marge Piercy, *Stone, Paper, Knife* (Pandora Press, London, 1983).

[7]  *Stove*
     *dear stove, the*
     *improbable arches of happiness,*
     what have I learned today?          (Wendy Mulford[20]: *The Hard*)

The punctuation (a matched pair of commas) helps to indicate co-referentiality here, but the knowledge that such emotional vocative appeals to more than one consciousness are relatively rare (*Jesus and Mary* perhaps being the exception and anyway being more often used in exclamatory than vocative mode) draws the reader towards the conclusion that 'the improbable arches of happiness' refers to the stove.

Although the commonest order of these metaphorical appositions in the data is literal phrase followed by metaphorical phrase(s), there are some cases where the order is reversed and the reader is led toward the literal version through one or more metaphorical phrases:

[8]  No. Let me have *this dust,*
     *these pale clouds dourly lingering, these words*
                    (Adrienne Rich: *Cartographies of Silence*)

There are no overt markers of apposition in [8] and in principle the three noun phrases could form a list of separate referents. However, the subject of the poem which explores relationships between lies, silence and words rather than weather or dirt (*dust* and *clouds*) predisposes the reader to interpret them metaphorically. The dust and cloud then become symbolic of the inaccuracy and inadequacy of words as Rich sees them.

Two other sub-groups of metaphorical appositions are signalled very clearly as being co-referential. The first is where the metaphorical version is postposed after the verb, either as an elaboration of the literal noun phrase as in [9] or of a pronoun as in [10], where the pronoun has an antecedent referring to 'the words' exchanged in an argument:

[20] From Wendy Mulford, *Late Spring Next Year* (Loxwood Stoneleigh, Bristol, 1987).

[9]            *scarlet runner beans*
       climb the bamboo trellises he's built for them,
       *crazy trees, like the ones that rose* . . .
                              (Bronwen Wallace[21]: *Houses*)

[10] how *they* natter, *dry birds*,
       in some empty room of the brain.
                              (Bronwen Wallace: *Gifts*)

In both [9] and [10] the co-referentiality of the phrases is established by the postposing of the second phrase - an impossibility for phrases which are conjoined. The other clearly appositive group of examples show the extent of their metaphorical versions by parenthetical pairs of commas or hyphens:

[11] Saw, for a moment, *the approaching tempest,*
       *A sudden animal raging across the woods,*
       Bend each tree as a current sways weeds in water.
                              (Jenny Joseph[22]: *February floods*)

[12] we noticed *a turtle – domed repoussé*
       *leather with an underlip of crimson –*
       as it hove eastward          (Amy Clampitt: *The Cove*)

[13]            *Two floral cats,*
       *enormous crimson walruses,*
       undulate on purple cloth     (Ruth Padel[23]: *Weekend child*)

In these examples, the second comma or hyphen is necessary in order for the clause structure to continue after the apposition.
   The final set of noun phrase examples included under the metaphorical heading are all potentially ambiguous because they have no obvious markers to indicate that they are not simply lists of coordinated noun phrases with separate referents. Extract [14], for example, comes from a poem which, apart from the last line, is made up of a series of noun phrases describing the sea:

21 From Bronwen Wallace, *The Stubborn Particulars of Grace* (MaClelland and Stewart, Toronto, 1987).
22 From Jenny Joseph, *Selected Poems* (Bloodaxe Books, Newcastle-upon-Tyne, 1993).

[14] *this buttermilk, this*
*herringbone of albatross,*
*floss of mercury,*
*déshabille of spun*
*aluminum,* (Amy Clampitt: *Marine Surface, Low Overcast*)

It is only the title of the poem that allows us to decode this series of apparently rather different noun phrases. And once the code is cracked, the relevance of each metaphor becomes clear: the opacity of buttermilk, the herringbone pattern of the waves and/or seabirds, the silver-grey colour of mercury and aluminum and so on.

Other examples may not be as sustained, but may be equally clearly designating the same referent, as in [15] where the referent, snow, is not mentioned, but has been well-established in many of the preceding lines of the poem:

[15]          We walk back
on *slipping fur, roan slush.*          (Ruth Padel: *Stepson*)

Whilst it is not one of my purposes to catalogue different structural types of apposition, two examples of clausal apposition which are metaphorical are worth considering:

[16] Our childhood wars have aged us
but it is the absence of change
*which will destroy us*
*which has crippled our harvest into nightmare*
. . .          (Audré Lorde: *Timing*)

[17] For those of us *who live at the shoreline*
*standing upon the constant edges of decision*
*crucial and alone*          (Audré Lorde: *A Litany for Survival*)

Just as in sequences of noun phrases, these clause sequences could refer to different actions, but are in fact clearly co-referential. We are asked to re-consider the meaning of 'destroy', by processing it through the harvest metaphor in [16]; and in [17] the reader's first assessment of what it means to 'live at the shoreline' is confirmed/denied or narrowed down by the explanatory second clause.

---

[23] From Ruth Padel, *Summer Snow* (Century Hutchinson, London, 1990).

NON-METAPHORICAL APPOSITION. Whilst there are many examples of metaphorical noun phrase sequences, there are also many which are not metaphorical. The data which forms the basis of this paper yielded six groups of non-metaphorical examples which seem to function in very general terms as literal 'versions' of the same reference. These all occur in surface structure as sequences of phrases of the same syntactic level and with the same syntactic function which also share their referent. Their distinguishing features are discussed below.

*Reformulations.*[24] Reformulations are closest to a re-wording of one phrase by another. In this group the first phrase is reworded by the second (and third etc.) without narrowing or generalising the focus and without recourse to metaphor. In everyday speech and functional writing many appositions would be of this sort and could have descriptive, pedagogical or self-correcting purposes as in the invented examples [18] to [20] respectively:

[18]  it was *a huge hole, an enormous crater*

[19]  it's *an alloy, two metals mixed together*

[20]  she's *a teacher, a higher education lecturer actually*

The rewordings under this heading are most typically based on linguistic knowledge and exploit semantic relationships such as hyponymy and (near-)synonymy in order to produce a phrase which is linguistically close to the original as well as sharing the referent. In poetic contexts, these rewordings are unlikely to be mundane paraphrases. The following extract, for example, is from a poem which points out how we all love to feel needed; our plants should not exactly die when we are away in hospital:

[21]  but there should be *some damage, some visible*
      *tangible pinchable tarnish of missing.*
                          (Marge Piercy: *Out of the hospital Peter*)

This apposition glosses what the writer means by 'damage' in the rather longer second noun phrase. There is a chatty feeling of self-correction or fumbling for words in the second phrase which is partly created by the sequence of three nearly synonymous adjectives: *visible*

---

[24] There are many slightly different uses of this term. I am using it in a narrowly-defined sense as described in this section.

*tangible, pinchable.* These mark out the senses with which the damage
should be perceived as being firstly sight and then also touch.

Another example which could be classified as reformulation shows
that even where near-synonyms are used, the rewording may add
information that is denied the reader by the first phrase. In *The Watch*,
Piercy draws our attention to the fact that many women at any one
moment will be waiting for:

> [22]  *the same sign of reprieve, the red*
>       *splash of freedom.*
>
> (Marge Piercy: *The Watch*)

Whilst 'sign'/'splash' and 'reprieve'/'freedom' are clearly intended to
be considered as partial synonyms here, the additional information
gained by the colour ('red') and the type of sign ('splash' of liquid) is
just different enough to decode the first noun phrase as referring to
menstrual blood which is here construed as confirming freedom from
pregnancy and motherhood.

In other cases, the reformulation may not be needed for decoding,
but may symbolise the meaning in a way that would not be possible if
the appositive phrase were missing:

> [23]  Though on days of thaw *a ponderous*
>       *icicle-fall, a more and more massively*
>       *glistening overhang*, gave birth to daggers
>
> (Amy Clampitt: *A Resumption*)

The subject of the clause in [23] consists of two phrases describing
the ice hanging over the edge of a building. The first is adequate from
a factual point of view, but the second symbolises the continuous
enlarging process by its long drawn out adverb phrase ('more and
more massively') modifying the adjective ('glistening') which in turn
modifies the noun ('overhang').

*Perceptions.* What I have called 'perceptions' are appositions in which
the phrases approach the referent from a different angle or from a
different viewpoint. Although they are similar to reformulations, they
may be very far from a re-wording in the usual sense.

> [24]       The thought
>       *of those thousands and thousands of stories –*
>       *the crush and babble of other minds –*   (Jo Shapcott[25]: *Volumes*)

[25] From Jo Shapcott, *Phrase Book* (Oxford University Press, Oxford, 1992).

The second phrase in [24] cannot be seen as a linguistically in-formed paraphrase of the first. As a definition of 'stories' it is unusual in that it primarily shows the writer's feeling of being oppressed by them which is a rather negative attitude.

In other examples where one of the terms is a single noun, the second phrase may read very much like a definition, though it is usually from a very personal viewpoint:

[25]             I thought forever
        came with *words, the hateful things
        we never took back,*             (Bronwen Wallace: *Benediction*)

Here, Bronwen Wallace is re-defining 'words' as equivalent only to the harsh words of an argument. Another similar extract, [26], further illustrates the way in which this type of apposition operates to re-define words appropriately in the context:

[26]  clings to his feet like *mud,*
      *something he must wash off*
      *before it can slow his progress*
                            (Marge Piercy: *The man who is leaving*)

In this poem Piercy has set up the simile which likens a woman's entreaties to a man not to leave her with, of all things, mud. Having established the comparison, she then uses a noun phrase in apposition to define exactly in what way the simile is appropriate. It reads as an unusual and personal definition of 'mud'.

The group of appositions categorised as 'perceptions' are like a literal version of metaphors. They often provide a surprising or new way of looking at something:

[27]  *one tough missed okra pod* clings to the vine
      *a parody of fruit cold-hard and swollen*
                            (Audré Lorde: *Walking our Boundaries*)

In this example, Audré Lorde evokes the feeling of a missed oppor-tunity, in this case that of harvesting the okra pod. The second noun phrase of the apposition adds both a descriptive dimension ('cold-hard and swollen') and a personal one; the gardener is 'teased' by the 'parody' of a fruit which looks right, but which she knows to be inedible.

*Generalisations.* Generalisations are a group of examples where the first, specific noun phrase is followed by a general phrase which places the specific referent in a general category:

[28] *Tears* wait in my eyes,
  *little accidents ready to happen.*   (Marge Piercy: *Ragged Ending*)

In [28], Piercy gives the tears a more general gloss in the second noun phrase. The effect is at least twofold: the reader is made aware that there are also other 'little accidents' which happen in life, and some specific examples may be derived from the second phrase. The reader is also led to consider the apparently contradictory nature of tearful eyes; the second phrase underlines the fact that we normally consider 'accidents' to be unexpected, but these are 'previewed' by the tears.

Whilst some generalising appositions invoke the general category in such a way that other members of that category are weakly implied, other examples may use a general phrase to explain the first phrase in some way, as in [29]:

[29]    The community of mallards,
    which the dog chases, not to catch,
    but for *that lift of wings to water,*
    *the power of making things happen.*      (Ruth Padel: *Foreigners*)

Here, the dog's motivation in chasing the ducks is interpreted by the poet as being an instance of the desire to exercise power over things. The general category may allow the human reader to empathise more readily with the dog, by invoking other members of the category which are more likely to motivate human beings.

The examples of generalisation given so far have only one specific example of a general category. There are some, however, which use an appositive noun phrase to 'sum up' the common elements in a list of phrases with different referents:

[30] If so, we were in the house, *the dark of it,*
    *the wood-framed double hung windows with no*
    *pulleys, post-war cheapness.*          (Erin Mouré: *Rain 6*)

Whilst the dark and the windows are clearly not comprehensive in describing the 'post-war cheapness', they are two indicative features which are intended to evoke the atmosphere summed up by the general phrase.

Some generalisations, however, rather than causing the reader to envisage other examples of the category, seem to be claiming that the specific example is the prime, or only, member of that group:

[31]  Always *the same beginning:*
      *words and the cells that make them*
      *all that will carry us*
      *into the future.*                    (Bronwen Wallace: *Departure*)

This is either a non-co-referential list (see the section on 'happy ambiguity' below) or the two phrases are intended to be read as co-extensive, even though the second phrase sounds much wider in its apparent reference. I favour the second reading myself, in which case Wallace is making a strong claim for the power of language, namely that it shapes our destiny.

*Narrowing.* Narrowing could be seen as the reverse of generalisation; the second phrase will usually be a detailed and more specific description of the same referent.

[32]  *halving the odds on immediate decay, keeping*
      *a firm straight back well into middle age*
                                           (Jo Shapcott: *Shopping*)

Here the first noun phrase introduces the topic of putting off the inevitable ageing process, and allows for a range of weak implicatures covering the variety of ways in which this may be achieved. The reader may start to envisage what 'halving the odds' might mean in practice, but the second phrase is responsible for narrowing the focus down to a specific, but undramatic strategy, 'keeping a firm straight back', and the effect is dampening.

Narrowing may achieve a number of poetic effects, although the interpretative process may well be very similar in each case. In [33], for example, Bronwen Wallace first of all gives us the broad outline of the father's dissatisfaction with his past, and then elaborates, so that our imagined version of 'the history he hated' is confirmed and/or denied:

[33]  his city life's the instrument
      that pries the memory loose
      from *the history he hated, the narrow*
      *caked path from pasture to barn*

*and the blistered sun at his neck*
*day after day.*                    (Bronwen Wallace: *Food*)

The man's history is described by two noun phrases which symbolise, by their timelessness, the enduring effect of a past that is only
apparently behind him.

A similar example gives the reader the general category of 'childhood' to begin with, but soon undermines those implicatures that this
word might evoke, by defining the childhood in very specific and
material terms:

[34]  then one night
      our father dying upstairs

      we burned *our childhood, reams of paper*          (Adrienne Rich)

*Exemplification.* Exemplification is related to narrowing, in that there
is usually a general category followed by at least one specific example.
Unlike narrowing, these examples seem to be truly representative of
the category, with no implication that there is only one member of
the group:

[35]     *whatever innocent object*
         *I touched, doorknob or light switch,*    (Marge Piercy: *The Weight*)

The exemplification in the next extract [36] has two levels. First,
there is a general category of things 'we learn to rely on', which is
followed by two more narrowly defined examples of what we rely on
('the smaller stratagems' and 'whatever works'). These three noun
phrases are followed by two highly specific examples of what those
stratagems might be:

[36]     You can call it a choice
         if you want, but that doesn't change
         *what we learn to rely on,*
         *the smaller stratagems. Whatever works.*
         *The socks in their neat balls, tucked on the right*
         *side of the drawer, the iris coming up each summer*
         *in the south bed.*
                         (Bronwen Wallace: *Joseph Macleod Daffodils*)

*Contrasts.* In some noun phrase sequences in the data, one noun
phrase would be used as a negative descriptor of the other. These

share reference in that they appear to be increasingly accurate descriptions of the same referent. This could, therefore, be seen as a special case of reformulation:

[37] I have been waking off and on
     all night to *that pain not simply absence but*
     *the presence of the past* destructive
     to living here and now.                    (Adrienne Rich: *Splittings*)

The use of opposites such as 'presence' and 'absence' are indicators that these are related very closely to the group called reformulations, which are linguistically-based rewordings.


## Happy ambiguity

This study started out with a hypothesis that one of the features of feminist style would turn out to be a tolerance of, even a delight in, the possibilities of ambiguity for interpretation. This section will examine those examples of noun phrase sequences which seem to support the hypothesis.

Whilst there may well be different ways of categorising those examples which were discussed in the last section, they are, at least, all relatively transparent in their interpretation. The metaphor section has already hinted that there are some cases where the co-referentiality of the noun phrases in sequence is not easily established and where, consequently, there is ambiguity between coordination and apposition.

The noun phrases listed in [14], for example, are clearly only co-referential (and thus appositive) once we interpret them metaphorically as referring to the marine landscape being described in the poem. A very similar example, but one which I cannot so confidently categorise as apposition is the list in [38]:

[38] *cold nights on the farm, a sock-shod*
     *stove-warmed flatiron slid under*
     *the covers,*
            (Amy Clampitt: *On the Disadvantages of Central Heating*)

The reader will probably conclude that these, and the many other noun phrases in the list, are clearly part of Clampitt's definition of the 'disadvantages of central heating', because they have disappeared with the arrival of such luxuries. However, they do not describe the disadvantages metaphorically, they are rather examples of what has disappeared and could hardly be seen as anything other than a list, in other words a conjoined sequence.

Another example which works similarly, but in a very different context is [39]:

[39] defies the is
            in silence of
                        *star*
                        *planet*
                        *galaxy*
                        *red dwarf*
                        *red shift*
                        *black hole*        (Marlene Nourbese Philip)[26]

Many of Philip's poems deal with silence – and this one seems paradoxically to be trying to define silence using words, which by their nature end silence. Just prior to this extract, Philip tries to break away from poetic tradition by rejecting simile as too 'noisy', presenting instead the above list of words referring to astronomical phenomena. The words stand starkly on the page, with connotations of deep space echoing around them. Whilst these nouns and noun phrases are clearly a list, not an apposition, they each perform the function of being an example of silence and to this extent are almost co-referential.

Other poems by Philip also use lists. But she has a range of uses for the list, which in some cases comes much closer to being appositive. In [40], for example, the use of closely-related words from the same lexical field may leave us uncertain whether they are intended to be synonymous or not:

[40]                    more
        than absence of
                    *tongue*
                    *language*
                    *speech*
            *of word*
                    is silence            (Marlene Nourbese Philip)

[26] From Marlene Nourbese Philip, *Looking for Livingstone: An Odyssey of Silence* (The Mercury Press, Toronto, 1991).

Here, Philip gives us a negative definition of silence, denying the popular notion that it simply amounts to a lack of speech. The way this list seems to work is that it plays on the polysemous sense of these very general lexical items to emphasise what they have in common. Thus 'tongue' may be interpreted as a body part until the reader reaches 'language', when 'tongue' can be reinterpreted as synonymous with 'language' in its countable sense (e.g. as in 'How many languages do you speak?'). The word 'language', in turn, loses this countable sense when the reader reinterprets it to mean the more general phenomenon of human communication as in 'speech'. The final part of the list adds 'word', used unconventionally as a mass noun, to name the phenomenon being described as the antithesis of, but not the defining feature of, silence.

In [40], it seems, both conjunction and apposition may be seen as legitimate interpretations. Philip may be defining 'word' as all of these things (conjunction) or she may be equating them all as being synonymous with 'word' (apposition). Or both. It is also possible to interpret the appositive possibility in terms of the spoken language where such strings of near-synonyms are seen as increasingly accurate attempts to find the right expression.

Other examples of noun phrase sequences may also look like lists, but hide a complicated relationship between the items on the 'list'. The five noun phrases in [41], for example, are superficially a conjoined list with the fourth and fifth phrases introduced by 'and' and 'or' respectively:

[41] We need to grasp our lives inseparable
from *those rancid dreams, that blurt of metal,*
*those disgraces,*
and *the red begonia perilously flashing*
*from a tenement sill six stories high*
or *the long-legged young girls playing ball*
(Adrienne Rich: *Love Poems I*)

In the context of this poem, these noun phrases take on a different complexion. Rich is claiming that we ignore at our peril the connection between pornography and our lives. The realisation that the first three noun phrases are probably reformulations of 'pornography' (pornographic films in particular) shows the reader that these three are in apposition (have the same reference as well as the same syntactic function) but that the other two phrases (depicting 'ordinary life') are conjoined with this appositive sequence. The effect is to simultaneously appear to conjoin those things that Rich is claiming are inextricably linked (i.e. pornography and ordinary life) whilst at the same time distinguishing them by setting them on either side of the conjunction 'and'.

There are a number of other examples in the data where the noun phrases in sequence could be both conjoined and in apposition. In [42], Audré Lorde is exploring her relationship with her parents:

> [42] I name you both the *laying down of power*
> *the separation I cannot yet make*
> *after all these years of blood*          (Audré Lorde: *Sequelae*)

The two noun phrases here both function as object complements of the verb 'name'. The reader could equally see them as defining each other (apposition) or as two aspects of the 'name' being assigned to the parents (conjunction). Either the parents are seen as the cause for her lack of power *and* as an adjunct from which she cannot separate, or they are seen as the lack of separation which causes her lack of power. The two interpretations may both be correct and anyway are not very different. The structural vagueness is not important.

In another example [43], Lorde addresses a friend who has been through some unnamed trauma:

> [43] I felt you wanting
> to mourn
> *the innocence of beginnings*
> *that old desire for blandness*.
> (Audré Lorde: *In Margaret's Garden*)

The two noun phrases here are difficult to categorise. They could be different perceptions of the same experience (equivalent in meaning) or the second could be a generalisation from the first. Equally they could be conjoined phrases with separate reference. In the realm of feelings and abstract ideas, reference and equivalence are very difficult to define. Is the 'innocence' a specific example of the 'desire for blandness' or are they two separate things being mourned? And does the answer make any difference to the reader's response to the poem? I suggest not.

Some of the examples discussed earlier were interpreted as clear examples of apposition, even though they appeared structurally ambiguous. These were usually from poems whose context made it very clear when equivalence was being proposed or when a metaphorical interpretation was appropriate.

Other examples, which look superficially like lists, could be interpreted as appositions on the basis of a specific kind of world knowledge. When an audience is assumed to share certain perceptions with the writer, these assumptions may be taken as the underlying ideology of the text and may affect the 'reading' of the work. In [44], for example, Philip produces an apparent 'list' of phrases referring to a woman:

[44] *bitch-white*
> *nigger-woman*
*black*
> *Victoria*
*Queen or Jemimah*
*whore-wife*
*virgin-slut*                                           ([Marlene Nourbese Philip)

These phrases lack clear boundaries, so that the reader may be unsure, for example, whether or not 'bitch-white' is pre-modifying 'nigger-woman' and whether 'black' stands on its own or as a modifier to 'Victoria'. This structural ambivalence in itself might lead the reader to take the phrases as co-referential. Feminist ideology would share the text's proposition that 'whore' and 'wife' are closer to being synonyms than the opposites they are usually perceived as and would extend this common-sense knowledge (too basic to be seen as an interpretation) to other phrases such as 'Queen or Jemimah'. The effect is to equate the phrases as if they are in apposition.

A similar example, which depends partly on world-view, is found in extract [45]:

[45] Now I must write for *myself  for this blind*
*woman scratching the pavement   with her wand of thought*
*this slippered crone   inching on icy streets*
*reaching into wire trashbaskets   pulling out*
*what was thrown away   and infinitely precious.*
> (Adrienne Rich: *Upper Broadway*)

The usual structural ambiguity pertains here: there is a pronoun, 'myself', followed by two noun phrases with apparently different reference. The identification of these drop-outs with the narrator (= poet?) rests on a number of shared assumptions that underlie feminist (and other) ideologies. These assumptions include the notion that the 'self' is not a transparent unity for each individual, but that people are composite (bundles of psychological and historical features) and through their shared characteristics they are also partly identified with others. Thus the three women in the extract may at the same time be 'separate' individuals and also three manifestations of woman (even historical predictions to what could be the fate of any woman).


CONCLUSION

This study was based on an initial hypothesis that although feminists might hanker after a tradition of language which 'started from some-where else', in practice women's use of language in poetry had to draw on the resources available, exploiting most often those features of language which most clearly reflect women's experience (this being no unitary phenomenon itself, of course).

A more specific hypothesis about the language of women's poetry concerned the nature of those features which seemed relevant to a 'women's language'. These were thought to include many of the fea-tures most readily exploited by contemporary women poets which seem to allow for a vagueness or plurality of interpretation often caused by the use of loose syntactic structures. The specific example of a loose syntactic structure chosen for study was the noun phrase sequence, whether conjoined or appositive or ambiguous/fluctuating between the two.

Clear examples of apposition can be categorised according to their function and their interpretation in terms of weak implicatures and relevance can be explored. The group of ambiguous/vague examples studied here illustrate the use of apposition and conjunction com-bined as an expressive device. It is interesting to note that the range of feminisms represented by the poets studied diminished considerably when this last type of 'happily ambiguous' examples was reached. The examples in this section (there are many more) were all from poetry by Philip, Rich and Lorde, all very well known for their radical feminist views.

The frequent use of apposition, I would suggest, is a hallmark of women's contemporary poetry and its use as a loose syntactic structure to provide a range of interpretation is most evident in feminist poetry. This structure could be seen as part of a linguistic description of a 'woman's sentence'.

No one lives in this room
without confronting the whiteness of the wall
behind the poems, planks of books,
photographs of dead heroines.
Without contemplating last and late
the true nature of poetry. The drive
to connect. The dream of a common language.
      (Adrienne Rich: *Origins and History of Consciousness*)

# Women, Men and Words: Lexical Choices in Two Fairy Tales of the 1920s

## LOUISE SYLVESTER

IN THIS STUDY I intend to examine some of the lexical choices within a particular conceptual field made by Eleanor Farjeon and Walter de la Mare in fairy tales they published in the early 1920s. The decision to compare vocabulary employed by these two writers stems from an interest in the question of gender and the use of language and from a desire to discover if linguistic usage in writing can be examined in the same way as women's and men's speech is analysed in the studies presented in, for example, *Women in their Speech Communities*.[1]

*The Glasgow Historical Thesaurus of English*, on which my analysis is based, will include almost the entire vocabulary of English from Old English to the present day arranged conceptually, and within each conceptual group chronologically, so that each sense will appear with its dates of usage in the language.[2] In it, for example, the semantic field *Expectation* is shown to consist of eleven sub-categories: Expectation, Prediction, Surprise, Disappointment, Hope, Trust, Fear, Despair, Caution, Courage, and Rashness, with further sub-divisions within each category. Words to be found in the vocabulary making up these sub-categories play a central part in the language of the stories selected for comparison: Walter de la Mare's 'The Lovely Myfanwy' (*Broomsticks*, 1925), and Eleanor Farjeon's 'The Mill of Dreams' (*Martin Pippin in the Apple Orchard*, 1921). Words from this conceptual field link many themes in the stories: the expectation of loss on the part of fathers; the lack of expectation of freedom on the part of

---

1 Jennifer Coates and Deborah Cameron, eds., *Women in Their Speech Communities* (Longman, London and New York, 1988).
2 *The Glasgow Historical Thesaurus of English* (Oxford University Press, forthcoming). More information can be found in T.J.P. Chase and C.J. Kay 'Constructing a Thesaurus Database', *Literary and Linguistic Computing*, 2 (1987) 161–163; C.J. Kay 'The Historical Thesaurus of English', *LEXeter '83 Proceedings*, ed. R.R.K Hartmann (Tubingen, 1984), pp. 87–90; J.A. Roberts, 'Some Problems of a Thesaurus Maker', Alfred Bammesberger, ed., *Problems of Old English Lexicography: Studies in Memory of Angus Cameron* (Verlag Friedrich Pintet, Regensburg, 1985).

daughters; their fear at the moment of appearance of men who may become their lovers, and at the moment of meeting them; the fear of loss on the part of the young women; and the fears and necessity for courage that surround their reunions with their lovers.

The question of whether or not men and women use language differently is singled out by Deborah Cameron in *Feminism and Linguistic Theory* as a primary area of investigation for proponents of feminist language theory. She links this question with another, the possible silencing of women by a language in which there is not room for the expression of their experience: 'is this the "oppressor's language", within which we cannot articulate our experience as women?'[3] In *A Room of One's Own* Virginia Woolf discusses the main difficulty faced by early nineteenth century women novelists. Woolf illustrates a sentence she finds typical of the prose of such novelists as Thackeray, Dickens and Balzac, commenting:

> That is a man's sentence; behind it one can see Johnson, Gibbon and the rest. It was a sentence that was unsuited for a woman's use. Charlotte Bronte, with all her splendid gift for prose, stumbled and fell with that clumsy weapon in her hands. George Eliot committed atrocities with it that beggar description.[4]

Does Woolf envision a different kind of writing produced by a woman freed from the constraints of the inherited prose sentence? Or are we to dismiss her judgement on grounds of reception: what appear to her as awkward stumblings might be read as the deliberate articulation of the difficulties inherent in expressing female experience at a time and in a mode unfitted for women's use. Woolf had in mind periodicity rather than lexical choice. I think it is extremely interesting, however, that she has a sense of the difference between the ways in which women might wish to express themselves, and the modes available to them in this period; she notes that 'since freedom and fullness of expression are the essence of the art, such a lack of tradition, such a scarcity and inadequacy of tools, must have told enormously upon the writing of women.'[5]

There is a sense in which separating the questions of difference and

3  Deborah Cameron, *Feminism and Linguistic Theory* (Macmillan, London, 1985), pp. 6–7.
4  Virginia Woolf, *A Room of One's Own* (Hogarth Press Ltd., 1929, repr. Granada Publishing Ltd., 1977), p. 73.
5  Ibid., p. 73.

alienation results in the presentation of a false dichotomy along the lines of reception. If we try to establish how men and women use language differently, the very examination of difference inevitably implies a deviation from norms of use, leading us to try to isolate how it is that women use language and whether or not we can talk about a 'women's language', or a female mode of language use. I hope that an examination of some of the lexical choices made by a male and a female writer writing within the same genre will provide a strategy for exploring the notion of difference.

The decision to focus on Farjeon and de la Mare was influenced by a number of factors, not least the period in which they were writing. In her study of British women novelists *A Literature of Their Own*, Elaine Showalter considers the literature of the generation of women novelists born between 1880 and 1900 to have entered a new phase which she calls 'a Female phase'; the way that she considers the literature of this period seems paradoxical: she says that it is a phase of 'courageous self-exploration' but that it carried with it 'the double legacy of feminine self-hatred and feminist withdrawal'.[6] She suggests that the women of this generation of writers seemed to cope with their dual roles as women and as professionals, enjoying professional and sexual fulfilment, while at the same time in their literature they rejected male society, masculine culture and the physical experience of women, and were retreating towards androgyny; although she notes that at the time the new female aesthetic was seen as women's culture emancipating itself from male domination.[7] Toril Moi criticizes Showalter's approach to literature for the way in which it draws upon feminist research in history, anthropology, psychology and sociology, to the virtual exclusion of the text. She suggests that for Showalter the text has 'disappeared', that it transmits human experience in a transparent fashion so that the only influences that constitute the text are extra-literary.[8] Even if Moi's criticisms are accepted, Showalter's insistence that the period following the First World War reflects a significant shift in the literary consciousness of women writers is still of interest. Most importantly for the purposes of this study, and despite what Moi has called her 'fear of the text and its

6 Elaine Showalter, *A Literature of Their Own* (Virago, London, 1977 revised 1982) p. 32.
7 Ibid., pp. 20 and 32–33.
8 Toril Moi, *Sexual/Textual Politics* (Methuen, London and New York, 1985), p. 78.

problems', Showalter notes that the new feminist aesthetic was ap-
plicable to language at the level of lexis as well as to ideas:

> After the war, women novelists . . . began to develop a fiction that
> celebrated a new consciousness. The female aesthetic applied fem-
> inist ideology to language as well as to literature, to words and
> sentences as well as to perceptions and values. (p. 240)

Showalter draws attention to Virginia Woolf's delight in what she
saw of women's fiction in 1929: 'It is courageous; it is sincere, it keeps
closely to what women feel. It is not bitter. It does not insist upon its
femininity. But at the same time a woman's book is not written as a
man would write it.'[9] Although Showalter identifies the period as one
in which the relations between the sexes were an aesthetic issue: that
is, that women at this time were searching for a female language or
mode of expression, she also suggests that in the period after the First
World War some of the best men and women writers were pursuing
similar aims 'yet no reader would mistake one for the other mainly
because their verbal territories scarcely overlap'[10] Showalter has thus
indicated that there were, and are, perceived differences in the way in
which men and women were writing at this period, and it seems from
the quotation above that the differences may be located in the area of
vocabulary choice. No precise textual analysis has led to her conclusion, but she points a way forward in her article 'Feminist Criticism in
the Wilderness': 'The appropriate task for feminist criticism, I believe,
is to concentrate on women's access to language, on the available
lexical range from which words can be selected.'[11] Perhaps a comparison of some of the lexical choices made by a male and female writer
working in the same genre in this period, and examined in the context of the available range of expressions which the Thesaurus arrangement of vocabulary allows us to do, may offer some clues.

Walter de la Mare and Eleanor Farjeon were born in 1873 and 1882
respectively. Farjeon's father was a writer of novels and plays which
were at one time extremely successful and she entertained no other
idea than that of following her vocation of writing. At the age of

9   Virginia Woolf, 'Women and Fiction' (1929) in Women and Writing (The
Women's Press, London, 1979), quoted in Elaine Showalter, op. cit. (1977),
p. 241.
10   Elaine Showalter, ibid., p. 241.
11   Elaine Showalter, 'Feminist Criticism in the Wilderness', Elizabeth Abel,
ed., Writing and Sexual Difference (Harvester, 1982) p. 225.

about twenty-four and after the death of her father she was living in
the family home and continuing to try to write, though she considered that for most of the time the pen was 'idle' in her hand.[12] In
contrast, Walter de la Mare while young worked for twenty years for
an oil company writing in his spare time. When he was thirty-five he
left the company and was awarded a grant from the Privy Purse to
allow him to devote the whole of his time to writing in recognition of
his literary stature and because of his ill-health. Each has been regarded perhaps primarily as a poet, but they both wrote plays, novels
and stories which were published independently or in collections
throughout the 1920s and after, and they both wrote for adults and for
children, although Farjeon's work for adults has received far less attention in recent years than that of de la Mare. In *Written for Children*,
John Rowe Townsend discusses the period in which they were writing,
noting that the psychological shock of the war was immense. He
considers that the best work of the post-war decade was mainly in
poetry, or fantasy, or poetic fantasy.[13] Perhaps it is not only the literature written by women whch shows signs of retreat from physical
experience noted by Showalter in this period.

## II

The scope of this essay does not allow a discussion of the morphology
of these stories, and the ways in which they can be classified as fairy
tales, but it is interesting to note that they conform to the specifica-
tions laid out by Propp for the beginning of a tale: 'A tale usually
begins with some sort of initial situation. The members of a family are
introduced.'[14] He enumerates the functions which succeed the initial
situation, II and III being 'An interdiction is addressed to the hero'
and 'The interdiction is violated.'[15] The patterns set up in their open-
ings and as the action unfolds fulfil our expectations of fairy tales.

[12] Annabel Farjeon, *Morning Has Broken: a biography of Eleanor Farjeon*
(Julia Macrae, London, 1986), p. 77.
[13] John Rowe Townsend, *Written for Children: an outline of English-language
children's literature* (Garnet Miller, 1965, revised edition, Kestrel Books,
1974, repr. Penguin Books), p. 163.
[14] V. Propp, *Morphology of the Folk Tale* (1968), second edition revised and
ed. Louis A. Wagner (University of Texas Press, Austin and London, 1975),
p. 25.
[15] Ibid., p. 26.

The stories begin by setting up situations that are almost exactly parallel: in de la Mare's 'The Lovely Myfanwy' Myfanwy lives 'in an old castle under the forested mountains of the Welsh marches' (p. 117),[16] and in Farjeon's 'The Mill of Dreams' Helen lives 'in a mill on the Sidlesham marshes' (p. 125).[17] Each lives alone with her father; Myfanwy's is 'morose and sullen' (p. 117) while Helen's is 'morose and welcomed no company'. (p. 126) Myfanwy is given everything 'but her freedom' (p. 117) and is 'her father's unransomable prisoner' (p. 118) while Helen's mill looks like a 'noble prison' and we are told that 'if the mill was a prison of dreams it was her prison too.' (p. 125) The fathers are morose and the daughters lonely for the same reason, the fathers' fear of the loss of their daughters; but the fear is handled differently by the two writers. De la Mare is explicit about Myfanwy's father's fear (the italics are mine):

> But ever since Myfanwy had been a child, a miserable *foreboding had haunted his mind*. Supposing she should some day leave him? Supposing she were lost or decoyed away? Supposing she fell ill and died? What then? The *dread of this haunted his mind day and night*. His dark brows loured at the very thought of it. It made him morose and sullen; it *tied up the tongue in his head* . . . He could trust nobody. He couldn't bear her out of his sight. He *spied, he watched, he walked in his sleep, he listened and peeped*; and all for *fear* of losing Myfanwy.
> (pp. 117–118)

We read how he gazes at her as if by mere looking he can keep her secure and prevent change, as if the world 'had never had course to *dread and tremble* at sound of the unrelenting footfall of Time.' (p. 118) and that her growing up added 'another and sharper *dread and foreboding*' (p. 119). When a lover does attract Myfanwy's attention, we hear that 'His *dreaded* hour was come' (p. 128). The feelings expressed by the term *dread* are, of course, those of expectation and fear. The noun *dread* appears in the semantic sub-category Expectation with the sense of 'The state of apprehensive expectation', a sense in which it is still current:

[16] Quotations from 'The Lovely Myfanwy' from Walter de la Mare, *Collected Stories for Children* (Faber and Faber Limited, London, 1947 repr. 1970), pp. 117–146.
[17] Quotations from 'The Mill of Dreams' from Eleanor Farjeon, *Martin Pippin in the Apple Orchard* (W. Collins & Sons & Co. Ltd., London, 1921 repr. 1922), pp. 125–172.

fear a1300—; suspicion a1340–a1700; suspect c1375–1620; dread c1400–; apprehension 1603–(1853)[18]

and it is the first term in the following sub-division 'To look forward with anxiety':

dread a1225—; fear a1300–1820; suspect 1509–1794 . . .

It has been in use from about 1200 to express the quality of terror or horror, and as a verb with the sense 'to be terrified' from about 1300 onwards. Its senses extend also to those words used of people and things which inspire fear:

*oga* OE; *ege/awe* OE–1330+1657; medusa 1390—; dread c1400—; scare 1530–1828; fear 1535–1667; fray-bug 1555–1671; frightment 1607+1649+1831; frighter c1611; frightfuls 1727; scarer 1740— . . .

The term *fear* which appears in all these groups is also used to express the cause of his distress: 'all for *fear* of losing Myfanwy' (p. 118), At the thought of this, for *fear* of it, he would sigh and groan within' (p. 119).

The fears of Helen's father in 'The Mill of Dreams' are not stressed and repeated by Farjeon: the father keeps his daughter as a servant, rather than as a companion. Fear is touched on as a motive for the father's attitude, but it seems to be placed deliberately in the background:

But the miller kept his daughter away from his custom. He never said why. Doubtless at the back of his mind was the *thought* of losing what was useful to him. (p. 127)

The term *thought* does appear in the first sub-division in the subcategory Expectation, 'The state or condition of mentally anticipating what is to come', first in use a1307–1677, and then revived as a

---

[18] A full classification of the semantic field of Expectation will be found in my *Studies in the Lexical Field of Expectation* (Rodopi Press, forthcoming). The dates are set out according to the conventions of the *Glasgow Thesaurus*: the first shows the first recorded usage of a sense, and the last the date after which it is thought to have fallen out of use. Brackets round a final date indicate that the word is likely still to be current; 'a' = *ante*, 'c' = *circa*.

modern term; but as the definition shows, it is carefully neutral in comparison with the emotional terms employed in the same context by de la Mare. Later in the story Farjeon offers a term with stronger connotations to express the father's feelings, and the notion of his fear is linked with a direct condemnation of his behaviour:

> Her father meanwhile grew harder and more tyrannical with years. There was little for him to *fear* now that any man would come to take her from him; but the habit of the oppressor was on him, and of the oppressed on her. (p. 139–140)

The words chosen to describe his thoughts and behaviour take us into a different conceptual field, one embracing notions of tyranny and oppression.

The writers of modern fairy tales must comprehend the expectations of readers aroused by reading any fiction which forms part of an acknowledged genre, and writers working within the same genre were chosen for this study because of the increased possibility of some overlap in their 'verbal territories'. Unless the work is simply devised as popular literature, however, the author will almost certainly be attempting something else as well. As Todorov points out:

> An additional difficulty besets the study of genres, one which has to do with the specific character of every esthetic norm. The major work creates, in a sense, a new genre and at the same time transgresses the previously valid rules of the genre . . . One might say that every great book establishes the existence of two genres, the reality of two norms: that of the genre it transgresses, which dominated the preceding literature, and that of the genre it creates.
>
> Yet there is a happy realm where this dialectical contradiction between the work and its genre does not exist: that of popular literature . . . the masterpiece of popular literature is precisely the book which best fits its genre.[19]

'The Lovely Myfanwy' was written specifically for children, while 'The Mill of Dreams' was originally intended, and was first published, for an adult audience. Neither appears to seek to transcend the fairy tale genre, although 'The Mill of Dreams' shows signs of wanting to do something different with it. At the level of lexical choice this can

---

[19] Tsvetan Todorov, *The Poetics of Prose*, trs. R. Howard (Basil Blackwell, Oxford, 1977), p. 43.

be interpreted in terms of the manipulation of core vocabulary within a specific semantic field.

The notion of 'core' vocabulary is notoriously difficult to define: as Ronald Carter notes, 'It is very much an intuitive notion even if its general validity has been commented on quite widely'.[20] He does, however, go on to indicate that 'core' vocabulary items are those which are more basic than others to the expression of meaning, and seems to suggest that languages require, at all levels, a complementary distinction between marked and unmarked features, and that degrees of expressivity would be extremely difficult to achieve without some 'neutral norm or unmarked set of features against which deviation can be measured.' (p. 39). One way of comparing the lexical choices made by de la Mare and Farjeon is to examine the extent to which they employ core vocabulary, and to which characters and emotions it is applied. De la Mare has clearly chosen to employ core terms in the vocabulary of Expectation and Fear to guide the reader into his story, and to express the emotions of the father-figure. Farjeon offers less information on this point, but has expressed the father's reactions in terms which take us outside the lexical groups of expectation and fear. She is thus employing vocabulary which differs from the terms in which the fear and expectation of the loss of a daughter might be expected to be couched, and is commenting on the father's behaviour in words which express the involvement and judgement of the author.

Inevitably a suitor arrives to penetrate the heroines' isolation. In both stories the meeting of the lovers is divided into two: in 'The Lovely Myfanwy' Myfanwy first sees her lover asleep, and in 'The Mill of Dreams' there is a knock at the door. It becomes clear from the vocabulary that de la Mare's heroine has, on some level, been expecting her lover:

> her heart told her that whoever and whatever this stranger might be, he was someone she had been *waiting for*, and even dreaming about, ever since she was a child (p. 122)

'Waiting for' is the first sub-division in the classification of the vocabulary of Expectation, following the notion of mentally anticipating what is to come, and is therefore more precise in its meaning of expecting, almost with the sense of expecting something specific. In

[20] Ronald Carter, 'A Note on Core Vocabulary', *Nottingham Linguistic Circular* 11 (1982), 39–50, p. 39.

'The Mill of Dreams' the knock at the door is the 'strangest thing that had ever happened' (p. 127), and clearly we have again moved outside the semantic field of Expectation. We hear that Helen's 'heart beat fast' (p. 127). The phrase appears in the Historical Thesaurus as a sense of the term 'have etc one's heart in one's mouth', in use from 1548 onwards as a physical expression of surprise. There is a shock implied at this moment in Farjeon's story. In de la Mare's story we find the term *astonishment* (p. 122), one which is found in the semantic category of surprise, and also of fear, in the sense of loss of self-possession through fear, but it is given to a squirrel, rather than to any of the main characters.

What Helen finds when she opens the door is 'a common lad'. It is now, however, that vocabulary expressive of fear, and which is core to the sense, comes into play. In Farjeon's story it is the lover who has expectations, although these are only that the girl will speak and smile:

> Helen *stared at him without answering* . . . The boy *waited for* her to speak, but as she did not, he shrugged his shoulders and turned away whistling his tune.
> Then she understood that he was going, and she ran after him quickly and touched his sleeve. He turned again, *expecting* her to speak: but she was still *dumb* . . . (p. 128)

He teases her and 'a faint colour came under her skin':

> "What *frightened* you? Did you think I was a scamp?"
> "I wasn't *frightened*," said Helen.
> "Don't tell me," mocked the boy. "You *couldn't get a word out*."
> "I wasn't *frightened*."

Farjeon has reserved the use of core terms for the climactic moment of the meeting between the lovers. The term 'frightened' appears at the beginning of the classification of the semantic category Fear, in use from a1721 onwards, but it also appears as 'fyrht' in the Old English period, in the medieval period as 'frighty', and in various later forms such as 'frighted' and 'frightsome'. The use of core vocabulary at this juncture perhaps stresses that this part of the story is its 'core'. It also serves to emphasize the normality of the situation in comparison with the future meetings of the lovers which, until the end of the story, are all situated in the realm of fantasy.

Helen's reaction of staring is found in the semantic category Fear:

the sub-division 'The condition of staring through fear' contains the lexical item *stare* c1400–1610+1904, as is Myfanwy's going cold, although the term there is *cool* 1605, found only once, in Shakespeare. Helen's and Myfanwy's other reactions appear to be covered by subdivisions in the category Surprise, where we find 'Temporarily speechless from surprise':

dumb a1300–; dumbfounded 1770–; dumbfoundered 1883.

and also *have etc. one's heart in one's mouth* 1548–. The honours in this case seem to be equally shared between the heroines, but, reversing the case of the descriptions of the fathers' fears, Farjeon has chosen to focus on Helen's fears and has employed both core and more expressive vocabulary to do so.

Linked to the examination of the use of core vocabulary in the two stories is the question of whether the vocabulary chosen tends to fall within a specific semantic field. In the case of the semantic field chosen for this comparison, it might tell us whether the emotions suggested by the situation at the beginning of the tale continue throughout, and whether the lexical field used to express those emotions continues to be viewed by the author as adequate for the rest of the tale.

'The Lovely Myfanwy' continues to be studded with words from the eleven lexical sub-categories of Expectation. We hear that Myfanwy's one sole longing and *despair* was the *wonder* if she will see her suitor again [Despair, Surprise] (p. 124); her mind is a medley of *thoughts* and *hopes* and *fears* [Expectation, Hope, Fear] (p. 124), she wishes to *warn* the stranger [Caution] (p. 124) for she is *haunted by the constant fear* [Fear] (p. 125) that he will have met with some accident, but she hears a crowd which is lost in *wonder* [Surprise] (p. 125) at his juggling. He is described as full of *courage* [Courage] (p. 126) and having come out in *hope* of seeing Myfanwy [Expectation, Hope] (p. 126). She watches in *wonderment* each *marvellous* piece of juggling [Surprise] (p. 128) and cries *Wonder of wonders!* [Surprise] (p. 129). Her father's response is to tell her that the world is full of '*adventurers*. [Rashness] This is a . . . *warning*, and *alarum* . . . we must be ten times more *cautious*; we must be *wary*' [Caution] (p. 124). In private, however, he sheds tears of 'rage and *despair*' (p. 128), and of 'jealousy and *despair*' (p. 131) and feels 'grief and *despair*' [Despair] (p. 131). Once he falls under a spell he suffers a *dreadful* change (p. 134), feels *horror*, is *dazed*, and stands in *dismay* (p. 135), the *flesh seemed to creep upon his bones* as he turned in *horror* and *dismay* . . . a *panic of fear* all but swept him away' because of his *dreadful* condition (p. 135). At last he is left 'breathless . . . *trembling* and *shuddering*' [Fear] (p. 136). Further evidence of similar clustering of vocabulary may be found by comparison with the classification of the lexical field Expectation, the complete semantic categories of which are listed above.

The vocabulary of the field of Expectation certainly appears in 'The Mill of Dreams', particularly in the fantasies of shipwreck where we hear of Helen's '*shaking* knees' (p. 141), that she '*shook* violently', is *shuddering* and is 'as *cold as ice*' (p. 142) leading her lover to feel *despair* (p. 142). In general, however, such clusterings are quite widely scattered in the story with a very few items of vocabulary from the semantic field Expectation repeated, interspersed with repetition of vocabulary from other semantic fields expressing the emotions and reactions of the couple. We find, for example, the vocabulary which expressed Helen's fear (p. 128) reprised: 'Tell me were you *frightened*? . . . Then why were you mum as a fish? . . . Why? why? why? – if you weren't *frightened*. Of course you were *frightened*' (p. 137). There are similar repetitions of vocabulary which falls into different lexical sets:

> '[. . .] I wish you'd look up.'
> 'No, not yet . . . presently. But you, did you look at me?'
> 'Didn't you see me look?'
> '[. . .] Oh, child, look up! . . .'
> She looked up. . . . (p. 134)

Thus Farjeon imitates the endlessly repetitive conversations of lovers, and similar repetitions appear throughout the story:

> 'You wept'
> 'Oh did you see? I turned my head away.'
> 'Why did you weep?'
> 'Because you thought I had misjudged you.'
> 'Then I misjudged you.'
> 'But I did not weep for that.'
> 'Would you if I misjudged you?' (p. 138)

Sometimes the repetition is used to mimic thought patterns rather than conversations:

> She was almost angry with him, but more angry with herself; but her self-anger was mixed with shame. She was ashamed that he made her feel so much, while he felt nothing. Did he feel nothing?
> (p. 158)

The lexical choices in the two fairy tales, while they occupy similar 'verbal territory' are thus seen to be quite different. A far greater proportion of the vocabulary of de la Mare's story remains within the bounds of the single semantic field of Expectation, including vocabulary from eight of its eleven sub-categories: Expectation, Surprise, Hope, Fear, Caution, Courage, Rashness. Farjeon's lexical choices, in a story within the same genre and with a similar plot, are spread over a wider range of semantic fields, for example those encompassing the notions of oppression and tyranny and tears and smiles, as well as the fear to be found in Expectation. She exploits far fewer of the semantic sub-categories which make up the semantic field of Expectation, and within this lexical field she exploits core vocabulary at one particular moment of her story, and then conjures this moment again by repetition of the same core terms. De la Mare offers core terms throughout his story, deriving from a greater number of the semantic sub-categories of the field of Expectation (see above).

We need to consider whether these variations in the way that the vocabulary of the stories is chosen can be ascribed to the differences in the gender of their writers. Clearly the differences in the lexical choices echo the different concerns of the two writers. De la Mare is writing a modern fairy tale, but it conforms to the fairy tale genre and fulfils our expectations of that genre. Examination of one semantic field reveals that he uses a large number of core terms, and that the vocabulary is taken from a number of sub-categories, but is largely confined to one semantic field. It is used to express the emotions of each of the three protagonists, although more space is devoted to the father and daughter. Farjeon has chosen the fairy tale genre but has attempted something different within it. Her central focus is the inner life of her heroine, and the emotions of the other characters, when glimpsed, are seen through her eyes. The story takes place almost entirely within the mind of the heroine and covers a period of twenty years. The vocabulary is taken from a number of semantic fields outside the one examined here, and reserves the use of core vocabulary from the field of Expectation for the first encounter between the lovers. The concerns of the story might thus be said to be female, as they deal entirely with the fantasy of one lonely young woman, but what of the structures of vocabulary employed? The story is held together not by the clustering of vocabulary from a particular semantic field, but by mesmeric repetition of a small number of chosen terms from a wide range of semantic fields. The resistance to systematic coherence through the use of a single semantic field might be claimed by Kristeva and other French feminist writers to be drawing on the semiotic order discernable through gaps and disruption and thus representing the femininity of the writer who is marginal to the symbolic order. As Cameron notes, for Kristeva 'anyone taking up the feminine subject postion retains strong links with the pre-Oedipal mother figure, and their language shows the influence of the chora [receptacle of childhood drives] to a marked degree.'[21] One could also posit Farjeon's repetitions as a treatment of lexis which echoes a child's repetition of a few chosen words. It is interesting to compare Kristeva's view of such narrative strategies with Showalter's critical response to Woolf's *A Room of One's Own*:

> What is most striking about the book texturally and structurally is its strenuous charm . . . The techniques of *Room* are like those of Woolf's fiction, particularly *Orlando*, which she was writing at the same time: repetition, exaggeration, parody, whimsy, and multiple viewpoint.[22]

As Toril Moi notes, Showalter gives the impression that Woolf's use of repetition etc. somehow distracts attention from the message that she wants to convey in the essay. Showalter appears to condemn the breaking up of what Kristeva terms the 'strict, rational defences' of conventional social meaning.[23]

Clearly there are dangers inherent in positing women's writing as the repository of all that is illogical and fragmented, since, as mentioned in the introduction, it may lead to categorizations of normative use and deviation. Nevertheless the examples shown here show clearly that the organization of the vocabulary in Farjeon's story differs from that employed by de la Mare, and reflects, I think, her attempt to stretch the genre of fairy tale to accommodate underlying themes and concerns quite different from those contained in de la Mare's more traditional tale. Close studies of a wider range of authors and stories within a single period and genre may uncover further confirmation of the differences in approach to lexical choice by female and male writers.

[21] Deborah Cameron, op. cit. (1985), pp. 125–126.
[22] Elaine Showalter, op. cit. (1977), p. 282.
[23] Toril Moi, op. cit. (1985), p. 2.

# From Queens to Convicts:
## Status, Sex and Language in Contemporary British Women's Drama

### ANNE VARTY

'THE SILENCE OF the dead can turn into a wild chorus. But the one alive who cannot speak, that one has truly lost all power'.[1] *The Love of the Nightingale* (1988), Timberlake Wertenbaker's feminist revision of the myth of Philomele and Procne, foregrounds many issues under discussion amongst those concerned with women's language, in particular the extent to which women are free to speak with their own voices. The purpose of this essay is to explore how female characters in drama written by women express their status of power or subordination. The discussion opens by taking as a paradigm a play in which the words are physically taken out of the protagonist's mouth, before considering further, less radical, examples to display a range of the representation of different social classes, sexual stereotypes, and linguistic strategies. Plays by Pam Gems, Liz Lochhead, Caryl Churchill, Sarah Daniels, and Andrea Dunbar, all of whom have their work staged in the subsidised sector of the British theatre, will be discussed.

The myth of Philomele's transformation into a nightingale is viewed by Wertenbaker as a story about how men take action to silence articulate women, and about how women may fight back. Wertenbaker's views on women's language are undoubtedly the most radical of the playwrights represented here. They meet accord with, for instance, the work of Mary Daly, Adrienne Rich and Dale Spender.[2] According to legend, Philomele is raped by her brother-in-law, Tereus, King of Thrace, who then cuts out her tongue so that she can neither tell what he has done nor seek justice. On arrival in Thrace she embroiders the story on a peplos for her sister Procne to understand what has happened. Procne, enraged, slaughters her son

---

[1] Timberlake Wertenbaker, *The Love of the Nightingale*, in *The Love of the Nightingale and The Grace of Mary Traverse* (1988; Faber and Faber, London, 1989), p. 36.
[2] See Deborah Cameron, *Feminism and Linguistic Theory* (Macmillan, London, 1985), pp. 91–95 for an account of positions held by these theorists.

Itys and serves him up to Tereus for dinner. Tereus then chases both women to kill them, but is prevented by a god who transforms all participants into birds: Philomele becomes a nightingale, Procne a swallow, Tereus a hoopoe and Itys a goldfinch. Of these only the nightingale has a voice which sounds through the western tradition of legend. In the Middle Ages two influential poems, *The Owl and the Nightingale*, and *The Virgin and the Nightingale*, written by monks, associate the nightingale with courtly love, a pleasing if sinful celebrant of erotic sensuality. This medieval connotation of the bird overlays the classical one, continuing through the English Renaissance and Romantic periods (including Coleridge's 'melancholy bird' and Keats's association of 'easeful death' with the bird's song) to the popular association today of the nightingale's song with the honeyed dusks of courtship. And even the classical myth, in transforming the raped and silenced woman to a bird with a beautiful song, perpetrates a grotesque amelioration of the tale of violence Philomele has to tell. Wertenbaker allows this tone of the ending to stand in the harmonious final scene of the play, but this is more a token of hope than recantation, and Tereus moreover has no speaking part.

The play presents a strictly hierarchical society in which the men rule and the women, however royal, serve. 'What can I say?' shrugs the Queen when her daughter Procne appeals against her arranged marriage, a war bargain, with Tereus.[3] There are two choruses, male and female, and this segregation reflects the distinct gender roles within the society. 'I have always believed that culture was kept by the women', states Tereus courting Procne.[4] He obviously believes that it is best left with them too, since when questioned later by Philomele on what Procne talks about he replies dismissively 'What women talk about'.[5] Tereus does not value the culture which he says is guarded by women, and desires no access to it. Robin Lakoff has put forward a linguistic argument which points to this kind of segregation: '[i]f she refuses to talk like a lady, she is ridiculed and subjected to criticism as unfeminine; if she does learn, she is ridiculed as unable to think clearly, unable to take part in a serious discussion: in some sense, as less than fully human'.[6] Much of the drama of the play arises from this

3   *Nightingale*, p. 5.
4   Ibid., p. 5.
5   Ibid., p. 16.
6   Robin Lakoff, *Language and Woman's Place* (Harper & Row, New York, 1975), rpt. in Deborah Cameron, ed., *The Feminist Critique of Language*. A

conflict. And it is Philomele's role to transgress the boundaries of acceptable female behaviour.

From the start she refuses to be bound by conventional proprieties. So, for instance, until the rape Philomele is chided for talking too much or out of turn: 'Don't say that, Philomele'; 'Quiet, Philomele!'; 'You ask too many questions, Philomele'; 'Hold back your tongue, Philomele'. But after the rape her generic identity supervenes upon her personal identity, and for the last time, she is ordered (by Tereus) 'Quiet, woman'.[7] What had been presented as a character trait becomes, from the male perspective, a generic offence. Dale Spender observes, '[t]he talkativeness of women has been gauged in comparison not with men but with *silence* . . . When silence is the desired state for women . . . then any talk in which a woman engages can be too much'.[8] And by addressing Philomele in this way, Tereus helps to promulgate the linguistic folkview that women are more prolix than men; this stereotypical view of women's verbal behaviour might justify as due punishment for disobedience the drastic action he takes next ('You should have kept quiet', he adds, afterwards).[9] The change in appellation from 'Philomele' to 'woman' also diminishes her social status; no longer an individual let alone a princess, even her nurse and servant asserts that she is 'nothing' after the rape.[10] By exchanging a particular for a general term Tereus asserts his domination of the language, and provides an example which confirms, for instance, Luce Irigaray's anxiety that a 'language which presents itself as universal, and which is in fact produced by men only, is this not what maintains the alienation and exploitation of women in and by society?'[11]

Tereus, until the rape, had commanded reverence, and Philomele's trust however misplaced; afterwards she rails against him in a lengthy tirade and imagined public address:

*Reader* (Routledge, London, 1990), p. 222. For a critique of this contentious position, see for instance, chapter 7 of *Women in their Speech Communities*, ed. J. Coates and D. Cameron (Longman, London, 1988).

7  *Nightingale*, pp. 2, 3, 26, 34, 35.

8  Dale Spender, *Man Made Language* (Routledge, London, 1980), p. 42.

9  For an account of the linguistic folklore about women's 'verbosity' see Jennifer Coates, *Women, Men and Language. A Sociolinguistic Account of Sex Differences in Language* (Longman, London, 1986), pp. 31–34. *Nightingale*, p. 37.

10  *Nightingale*, p. 40.

11  Luce Irigaray in interview rpt. in *Feminist Critique* ed. Cameron, p. 80, from *Ideology and Consciousness*, vol. 1 (1977).

Have the men and women of Thrace seen you naked? Shall I tell
them? Yes, I will talk.

. . .

You call this man your king, men and women of Thrace, this
scarecrow dribbling embarrassed lust, that is what I will say to
them, you revere him, but have you looked at him? No? You're too
awed. . . .[12]

She may conform to a stereotype of verbosity and emotionality, but
her assertiveness breaks the female mould and this is where her threat
lies: 'You threatened the order of my rule', he tells her, once the
tongue is out.[13] Speech here is so potent that a change in name (or
'calling') can bring about change in identity and perceived status. The
world portrayed here is one in which power is maintained, or gained,
by adroit command of language. Authoritative utterance becomes a
substitute for true utterance, and 'truth' is not discoverable by verbal
means. 'It was you or me', Tereus informs Philomele later, aware of
how her word against his could diminish him.[14] The social order, and
gender identity within it, are shown to be verbally constructed. 'I
don't know what she wants. She can no longer command me. What
good is a servant without orders? I will go', complains Niobe after
Philomele is silenced.[15] And it is precisely from this perspective, one
which accepts and depends on the existing social status quo, that
Philomele can be seen to bring the violation of her tongue upon
herself. She, after all, has violated the conventions of order by daring
to give verbal expression to her anger, and by challenging his regal
status.

This second mutilation of Philomele, which happens on stage,
stands as a theatrical metaphor for the rape and a kind of equivalence
is set up between the two events. Irigaray's definition of the female sex
as 'made up of *two lips*' may suggest the link between a woman's vocal
eloquence and her sexual power,[16] which are assaulted together in this
retelling of the myth. The violation of Philomele's tongue deprives
her not just of words but of access to an entire semiotic system. She is
forced to find alternative means of communication. In suffering this
compulsion she simply expresses in extreme form the senses of linguistic apartheid and verbal inadequacy experienced by the other women

12 *Nightingale*, p. 35.          15 Ibid., p. 36.
13 Ibid., p. 36.                   16 Iragaray, op. cit. (1977), p. 83.
14 Ibid., p. 37.

in the play. 'Where have all the words gone?' asks Procne, waiting for
Philomele to arrive from Athens with her husband, and longing to
share a linguistic community with her, remembering '[h]ow we talked.
Our words played, caressed each other, our words were tossed lightly, a
challenge to catch'. Members of her court, the female chorus, try to
comfort her by pointing to new, male, family ties. These Procne
rejects, 'I cannot talk to my husband. I have nothing to say to my
son'.[17] One of her ladies-in-waiting suffers equally from a sense that 'I
have trouble expressing myself. The world I see and the words I have
do not match'.[18] It is significant that Wertenbaker's female characters
are capable of language-independent perception; they are not, therefore, victims of linguistic determinism to the extent that Adrienne
Rich, for instance, argues. For her 'as long as our language is inadequate, our vision remains formless'.[19] For Wertenbaker, it is not that
language is an autonomous system strangely user-unfriendly to
women, but that men who rule the society do so partly by dictating
how language is to be used. The male hegemony deploys words to its
advantage and to the disadvantage of women, hardly even allowing
them the access of use. 'Overcoming the silencing of women is an
extreme act', states Mary Daly.[20]

   The constraints set on Philomele when she does talk illustrate this.
When she, Tereus and the Athenian court watch *Hippolytus*,
Philomele's conversation with her brother-in-law is checked by her
father, 'Philomele, you are talking to a king'. But Tereus is minded to
hear her out, 'And to a brother, let her speak, Pandion'. Amongst her
comments is an explanation about Phaedra's action, designed to
soothe Tereus' shock at the fact that Phaedra lied. 'It's the god', she
says, indicating that Phaedra cannot help herself.[21] These words
Tereus later throws back at Philomele to excuse his own action in
raping her, informing her that as she herself has offered this as a
reason before, she must recognise its force now. On another occasion
Philomele again wins permission from Tereus to speak; indeed, he

17 *Nightingale*, pp. 6, 7, 7.
18 *Nightingale*, p. 20. The confusion experienced by women as a result of
sexually segregated linguistic behaviour is described by Lakoff in *Language
and Woman's Place*, rpt in Cameron, ed., op. cit. (1990), pp. 221–23.
19 Adrienne Rich, 'Power and Danger', in *On Lies, Secrets and Silence* (Virago, London, 1980), p. 248.
20 Mary Daly, *Gyn/Ecology: The Meta-ethics of Radical Feminism* (Women's
Press, London, 1978), p. 1.
21 *Nightingale*, pp. 10, 12, 12.

orders her 'Come and talk to me, Philomele'. But when she asks questions which he cannot or will not answer he complains, 'I didn't ask you to grill me, Philomele. Talk to me . . .'.[22] Niobe, Philomele's servant, of course understands the difference between an imperative and an invitation: 'entertain his lordship' she prompts, when it becomes clear that Philomele understands 'talk' as conversation amongst equals and Tereus has already said that he is her brother. Her literal-mindedness is rapidly exposed as naive.

The male chorus (which, unlike the female chorus, is always designated as one voice) confesses, however bewildered, the male hand in semantic manipulation by pointing to the shift in the meaning of 'myth':

What is a myth? The oblique image of an unwanted truth, reverberating through time.
And yet, the first, the Greek meaning of myth, is simply delivered by word of mouth, a myth is speech, public speech. . . .
How has the meaning of myth been transformed from public speech to unlikely story?[23]

The mystery is not difficult to explain. Where a king can say to his sister-in-law before he rapes her 'fear is consent',[24] and afterwards cuts out her tongue because he objects to what she will tell his people, public speech is either duplicitous or not heard. Where men abuse the consensus about what words mean, Humpty Dumpty-like, as a means of abusing women, and women are deprived of speech altogether, why should credence be given to any public utterance?

The alternative semiotic system Philomele adopts when silenced is that of gesture. She constructs giant dolls, and manipulates them in the market place so that they act out the story of her rape. By chance Procne watches this performance, recognises her sister, and understands. Together and in cold blood the sisters take revenge against Tereus and men in general: Procne holds Itys, her son, while Philomele wields the knife to kill him. Once again, the women violate the male order, this time by performing an action which hitherto only the men had done. Gesturally this action echoes both the rape, and the mutilation of Philomele. The women's use of action to take power when discourse fails them suggests an equivalence between

22 Ibid., p. 16.                    24 Ibid., p. 30.
23 Ibid., p. 19.

action and speech which in turn invites the kind of analysis of speech that is alert to its status as action.

Speech act analysis can yield results that differ from the semantic or lexical analysis offered so far. For instance, if the vocabulary of the scene which ends with Tereus' mutilation of her tongue is considered, it seems that Philomele commits all the crimes. Flagrantly disobedient, she does not heed his imperative commands to silence, and she uses hyperbolical diction which has no literal application. Tereus is not literally a 'scarecrow', as she asserts, though he is a king, which she denies. And she, not he, predicts that the rape will be called (and dismissed) as 'high spirits', and the murder 'bravery'.[25] If, however, one examines the dynamics of the verbal exchange in different terms, then Tereus is manifestly at fault. He begins by violating the turn-taking conventions of conversation: Philomele asks questions which are not designed as rhetorical, and she pauses appropriately for him to reply. As Pamela Fishman argues, 'Questions are both explicit invitations to the listener to respond and demands that they do so. The questioner has rights to complain if there is no response forthcoming. Questions are stronger forms interactively than declaratives. A declarative can be more easily ignored'.[26] Tereus denies her a response, and forces her probing to continue.[27] This makes her speech seem to be hesitating bewilderment that is driven ever more inward, and insane. But then she does find her voice; she stops waiting for Tereus to explain, and her anger streams forth in accusation and questions which now are conspicuously rhetorical. And only then does Tereus respond, again inappropriately, with the command to silence. His loss of power, a consequence of his refusal to follow convention is confirmed by the fact that he has to resort to physical action in order to answer verbal action.

While few of the plays considered here depict sexually segregated speech communities, and the mutual damage incurred, quite so vividly as *The Love of the Nightingale*, related linguistic issues are nevertheless addressed. Women in verbal and political control are seen as

---

[25] Her verbal behaviour thus seems to confirm another piece of received wisdom about women's language put forward by Otto Jesperson about 'the fondness of women for hyperbole' in *Language, Its Nature, Development and Origin* (1922), cited by Jennifer Coates, op. cit. (1986), p. 19.

[26] Pamela Fishman, in D. Cameron, ed., op. cit. (1990), pp. 236–37.

[27] For a brief account of conversational turn-taking see Ronald Wardhaugh, *An Introduction to Sociolinguistics* (Basil Blackwell, Oxford, 1986), p. 289.

violating tacit conventions about how women 'should' behave, and if they do not adopt stereotypical male speech patterns they are shown casting about ineffectually for linguistic means to assert control without compromising their sex. Liz Lochhead's play *Mary Queen of Scots Got Her Head Chopped Off* (1987) presents a fight to the death between 'two queens in one island, both o' the wan language – mair or less'.[28] Lochhead marks the dialect distinction clearly between Queen Elizabeth's RP and Queen Mary's *'strange accent – a French-woman speaking Scots, not English, with, at the beginning of the play, getting subtly less as it proceeds, quite a French accent'*.[29] Mary is thus marginalised from the moment she opens her mouth, her shaky command of the language follows through to an unconvincing command of her Scottish subjects, and a complete incompetence in the affairs of State: 'I'm your queen. And in three years in this country I canna depend on any o' ye to show me royal respect as I am due, although in every way I try – (*Into tears*)'.[30] She is not the woman to break the English hegemony on the British mainland which applied then as now. Political incompetence is compounded by her unwillingness to put aside private, and stereotypically female, needs, in the interests of public office. Her first solution to the power struggle that must take place on her arrival is the childishly fanciful 'I wish that Elizabeth was a man and I would willingly marry her! And wouldn't that make an end of all debates!'.[31] Elizabeth, who plays a man's game, suppresses her own private needs for a partner, and uses Mary's desire for a husband as the first step towards manoeuvring her downfall. Elizabeth's personal decision to suppress an important aspect of herself is presented as necessary in a culture where women are not the 'natural' heirs to power. Elizabeth, in a private conversation with her maid (played by the same actor as Mary) reveals 'I said, Leicester, if I married you and we lay down together as King and Queen, then we should wake as plain Mister and Mistress Dudley. The Nation would not have it'.[32] Names are all important tokens of social status.

This self-censorship, the private dimension of her public persecution

---

[28] Liz Lochhead, *Mary Queen of Scots Got Her Head Chopped Off* in *Mary Queen of Scots Got Her Head Chopped Off & Dracula* (Penguin, Harmondsworth, 1989), p. 15.

[29] Ibid., p. 13.

[30] Ibid., p. 27.

[31] Ibid., p. 15.

[32] Ibid., p. 24.

of Mary, has for Lochhead (whose inspiration for the characterisation of Elizabeth was drawn from the public persona of Mrs Thatcher), a thoroughly contemporary application. Elizabeth's success is won at personal cost; her decision to divide public from private self is reflected linguistically by the contradictory utterances of her subconscious, exposed during a nightmare scene. 'Don't want – I want – Don't want to be Daddy's little princess. Yes!'.[33] Awake and conscious, Elizabeth is able to turn such verbally quixotic behaviour into a political strength. Carefully controlled syntactic ambiguity is exploited to maintain her personal and political innocence. Her last speech is typical:

> My subjects love me! I am the Virgin Queen! I love my good cousin Queen Mary and will keep her my honoured quest in all luxury in the lavish hospitality of my proudest castle. For her own safety.
> And my so-called 'wise advisers' would have to trick me before I would consent to sign a warrant for her death.
> Would have to trick me. Trick me. Trick me!
> (*Her manic repetitions begin to sound like instructions to invisible advisers . . .*)[34]

Every assertion here is false, where 'guest' means 'prisoner', and simply by the paralinguistic duplicity of induced hysteria (again, a stereotypically feminine way of protesting innocence), Elizabeth turns a conditional verb 'would have to' into an imperative, 'trick me'. So she both retains her 'virgin' purity and authorises the death warrant for her rival. Although ruthless and apparently 'male' in her desire for power, Elizabeth transforms her femininity into a type that governs successfully without resorting to male role-models either in behaviour or in speech. She thereby differs from the women in *Nightingale*, and is an exception to Lakoff's rule about the debilitating effects of sexual bilingualism.[35] Mary is not so canny.

*Queen Christina* by Pam Gems, written ten years earlier (1977), also turns historical subject-matter to contemporary effect, and presents a monarch female by nature and male by nurture. She is Christina (1626–1689), daughter of the Swedish king Gustavus Adolphus. Her

---

33 Ibid., p. 24.
34 Ibid., p. 63.
35 See note 6.

first adult appearance in the play is as a 'man', and the audience has as much difficulty to identify her as does her suitor:

> A beautiful young woman enters. She is wearing a simple but beautifully cut riding habit. Her pale ringlets fall about a beautiful but thoughtful face. She smiles as she approaches, and the PRINCE, enchanted, moves forward, smiling in delight.

> MAN (at the door): What's all this?

> He enters, a battered figure in hunting clothes. He slouches up to the young woman, moving louchely – he appears to be slightly crippled, or perhaps it is that one of his shoulders is out of true, giving him a swivelled, crooked appearance. He puts a familiar hand on the young woman's shoulder.

> Who the hell's this?

> . . .

> [the Prince reaches for his sword]

> Steady on . . .. steady on!

> . . .

> [the Prince draws his sword]

> . . .

> At least there's some spunk in him. (He thumps the PRINCE genially on the shoulder, sending him reeling, then turns to AXEL with a murderous face.) Some sort of joke?[36]

The 'beautiful young woman' (in fact Christina's lady-in-waiting) comes from the world of fairy tale, where the princess is a paragon of smiling passivity and charm; the 'prince', swift to defend his lady's honour, belongs equally to the realm of folktale. These figures, established by the stage directions, are easily recognised by the audience, just as the figures themselves seem readily to recognise each other. The 'man' cannot be so easily accommodated. Physically marginal, yet able to upstage the beautiful woman from the threshold of the stage; badly dressed, moving inelegantly, yet familiar with the beautiful woman, the 'man' can command the chancellor and challenge the suing prince. This figure does not conform to any type the audience might recognise, nor does he fit into a known court hierarchy. Only the adverb 'louchely' in the stage directions gives the obscurest hint about the sexual identity of the 'man'. His language functions as an

---

[36] Pam Gems, Queen Christina in Plays by Women. Volume Five ed. Mary Remnant (Methuen, London, 1986), pp. 18–19.

equally convincing disguise. Peremptory questions reinforced by swearing, unaccommodating reassurance ('steady on'), colloquial diction used in a formal situation ('spunk'), together with the casual rudeness of referring to a visitor in the third person, combine to make the character sound boorishly and stereotypically male according to standards of covert prestige.[37]

Only when the 'man' chooses to reveal her identity can the disguise be penetrated:

> He . . . she . . . that is to say, CHRISTINA, takes the PRINCE's nerveless arm and stands beside him in wifely stance. Even AXEL masks a momentary smile.
>
> CHRISTINA: You'll have to do better than this. I'm sorry, little fellow.[38]

The effect of this revelation is shocking, especially so since her 'masculine' disregard for verbal and behavioural proprieties does not alter. Queen Christina, like her father who commanded that she should be raised as a boy in the absence of a male heir, knows that a country, or empire, cannot be governed by one who observes the rules of feminine propriety. Only at her entrance did she occupy her physically 'correct' place on the periphery of the stage/court. Making her entrance, social positioning revealed in part by language, overrides her sexual place, thereby creating a destabilising effect in society (the prince draws his sword). Power, the playwright seems to suggest, has a masculine gender, the sexual identities of powerful women are correspondingly compromised, and the stability of the State is jeopardised. Christina, unlike Lochhead's Elizabeth, never finds an idiom with which to govern that does not conform to male stereotype. Paradoxically it seems that a woman in power who dispatches confused verbal signals is more effective and less threatening than a woman who utters unambiguous commands.

The Grace of Mary Traverse (1985) by Wertenbaker, set in the eighteenth century but no more a history play than Mary Queen of Scots or Christina, also exposes the discrepancy between the rules for the conduct of ladies' conversation and the semantic content of what

---

[37] For an account of the relationship between covert prestige and masculinity, see Coates, op. cit. (1986), pp. 73–4.
[38] Christina, p. 19.

that conversation might be about. The play opens with a lesson in conversational etiquette for women:

> MARY TRAVERSE *sits elegantly, facing an empty chair. She talks to the chair with animation.* GILES TRAVERSE [her father] *stands behind and away from her.*
>
> MARY TRAVERSE:  Nature, my lord. (*Pause.*) It was here all the time and we've only just discovered it. What is nature? No, that's a direct question. Perhaps we will not exhaust nature as easily as we have other pleasures for it is difficult to imagine with what to replace it. And there's so much of it! No, that's too enthusiastic. (*Short pause.*) . . . Oh dear, is that blue-stockinged or merely incomprehensible? . . . Whirlpools. Trees. Primordial matter. Circling. Indeed. Oh.
>
> (MARY *stops in a panic.* GILES TRAVERSE *clears his throat.* MARY *talks faster.*)
> . . .
> GILES:  You are here not to express your desires but to make conversation.
> MARY:  Can desires not be part of a conversation?
> GILES:  No. To be agreeable, a young woman must always make the other person say interesting things.
> MARY:  He hasn't said a word.
> GILES:  Ah, but he won't know that . . .[39]

Mary is as effectively gagged as Philomele, yet courtesy books and etiquette manuals in circulation during the last two hundred years show that this kind of training is not far-fetched.[40] Wertenbaker, however, uses the historical context and the comedy of the scene as alienating devices to expose tacit assumptions about stereotypical role play in male-female conversation, and in society at large, that operate today. Jennifer Coates observes, 'it seems that women put far more effort than men into maintaining and facilitating conversation',[41] Mary is learning the proprieties of upper middle class linguistic

[39] Timberlake Wertenbaker, *The Grace of Mary Traverse* in *The Love of the Nightingale and The Grace of Mary Traverse* (Faber and Faber, London, 1989), pp. 59–60.
[40] For an account of the conventions and proprieties governing women's speech over the last two hundred years, see chapter four of L.C. Mugglestone, *Talking Proper* (Oxford University Press, Oxford, 1994).
[41] Coates, op. cit. (1986), p. 154.

behaviour from her father; while all the rules are designed to keep
Mary in her place, i.e. to secure her a well-matched husband, and thus
to perpetuate a male hegemony, Mary learns her lesson more effectively than her father had bargained. 'It's my father who taught me to
talk, Sir. He didn't suspect he'd also be teaching me to think',[42] she –
now a prostitute – explains to a client who happens to be her father.

In scene two Mary is practising how to walk, and looks for approval
from her servant, Mrs Temptwell. A very different world view is
revealed:

MARY: . . . Do I look etherial?
MRS TEMPTWELL:   You do look a little ill, Miss Mary, yes.
MARY:   . . . I'm trying not to breathe.
MRS TEMPTWELL:   Oh yes. Your mother was good at that.
. . . She died of not breathing in the end . . . She was so quiet, your
mother, it took the master a week to notice she was dead. . .[43]

Unlike Niobe in *Nightingale*, the servants here see through upper class
pretension and enjoy an independence of spirit, if not of economy.
Mary rejects the speechless, weightless passivity to which her father
would have her aspire, and ventures out of the house, chaperoned by
Mrs Temptwell, under the pretence that this will 'improve [her] conversation'.[44] She never returns, and so crosses out of her proper social
sphere and experiments with, albeit downward, social mobility.
Throughout the play men are presented as being particularly suscep-
tible to the literal meaning of words, while women, often the victims
of this literal mindedness, are shown to be more cautious. One of the
first things Mary witnesses on leaving the house is a rape, in which
the man, Lord Gordon, is sexually stimulated by making his victim
beg for mercy: 'What delight! Say over and over again Lord Gordon
have mercy on me'.[45] Similarly, Lord Exrake (who doubles as Giles
Traverse), follows the condemned to the gallows in order to be comforted by their last words. This can have the effect of brainwashing,
presented like advertising: 'That's what a man said a few weeks ago.
Drink Olvitie. I've been drinking it ever since'.[46]

Mary, on the other hand, in crossing out of the threshold of her
father's house, defies convention, and learns to cut across the cant of

---

[42] *Mary Traverse*, p. 97.              [45] Ibid., p. 68.
[43] Ibid., p. 63.                        [46] Ibid., p. 128.
[44] Ibid., p. 65.

capitalism just as her servants had done. She takes to whoring as a means of supporting herself, in the course of which she encounters her father as a client to whom she can demonstrate that her conversation has indeed 'improved'. Finding himself about to be engaged by her in conversation he complains 'I want a woman, not a personality',[47] and on being told her identity, he rejects the possibility that she could be his daughter:

> MARY:  Is a daughter not a daughter when she's a whore? Or can she not be your daughter? Which words are at war here: whore, daughter, my? I am a daughter but not yours, I am your whore but not your daughter. You dismiss the my with such ease you make fatherhood a deed of possession, torn at will. Or is it your act of grace? An honour I can only buy with my graces? These discarded, I fall from your grace and free you of fatherhood because I disgrace you.[48]

In this more blatant context of sale and service such verbal dexterity is a painful reminder of the activity to which her father set her in his own home and under his own supervision. Her clear linguistic superiority suggests that social status might be more appropriately measured in terms other than those of birth, income or sex. She, like Philomele, challenges the authority by which names grant status.

Churchill's portrayal of the socially mobile woman in *Top Girls* (1982) charts the movement from working class to nouvelle riche, and deposits Marlene, the protagonist, in the same social position at the end of the play as Mary Traverse occupies at the beginning. Where Mary rebels, Marlene conforms. She assimilates with the verbal and behavioural patterns of the executive middle class male in order to achieve wealth and power. This conforms with the observations of the linguistic anthropologist Shirley Ardener, who argues that '[i]n any situation, only the dominant mode of the relevant group will be 'heard' or 'listened to'. And the 'muted groups' in any context, if they wish to communicate, must express themselves in terms of this mode'.[49] The last Act of the play shows Marlene in confrontation with her sister Joyce who stayed at home to rear Marlene's illegitimate

47 Ibid., p. 96.
48 Ibid., p. 98.
49 Shirley Ardener, *Defining Females* (1978), p. 20, cited in Cameron, op. cit. (1985), p. 105.

daughter as her own. Marlene taunts her with their political differences: 'Bosses still walking on the workers' faces? Still Dadda's little
parrot? Haven't you learned to think for yourself? I believe in the
individual. Look at me'.[50] Joyce may indeed voice and share her
father's politics, but Marlene's are not therefore less patriarchally
structured. She continues:

> I hate the working class/ which is what you're going . . . to go on
> about now, it doesn't exist any more, it means lazy and stupid. / I
> don't . . . like beer guts and football vomit and saucy tits/ and
> brothers and sisters . . .[51]

Talking over her sister's interjections (i.e. not turn-taking, like Tereus
in Nightingale) Marlene reveals linguistically that, while she believes
in the individual (herself) she, like Mrs Thatcher, does not believe in
'society' (herself in relation to others). By redefining 'working class', a
collective noun, as 'lazy and stupid', two adjectives, she shows how
language can change a substantive into a quality and she suggests how
it may indeed be true that the working class has ceased to exist. If it is
not recognised by those in power, and not heard by them either (both
of which are illustrated by Marlene's verbal behaviour here), its existence is politically threatened as is its ability to identify itself. Her
connotations of 'working class' are those clichés given by the tabloid
press, notoriously male-run and usually Tory in allegiance. Her subse-
quent protestation 'I want to be free in a free world' reflects the extent
to which she regurgitates the clichés of Thatcherism, when her professional success (managing director of an employment agency for
women) depends on putting price tags on the most insubstantial
qualities, and the certainty that nothing is free. Marlene's speech
patterns throughout illustrate a feature which Herbert Marcuse con-
tends is characteristic of capitalist society:

> The unification of opposites which characterises the commercial
> and political style is one of the many ways in which discourse and
> communication make themselves immune against the expression of
> protest and refusal.[52]

[50] Caryl Churchill, Top Girls in Plays: Two (Methuen, London, 1990), p.
138.
[51] Ibid., p. 139.
[52] Herbert Marcuse, One Dimensional Man. Studies in the Ideology of Advanced
Industrial Society (1964; Routledge & Kegan Paul Ltd., London, 1968), p. 90.

While *Top Girls* is specifically about the social opportunities available to women, *Serious Money* (1987) portrays the macho hub of the economic engine that runs the West, and feminist concerns are inferred rather than stated. Set in the City, women are either humiliated or assimilated. There is no way of being 'feminine' and operating professionally in this field:

> Terry: Are you Annie? Can you find this guy and give him a message?
> Annie: Mike who?
> Terry: Hunt.
> . . .
> Annie: I'm looking for Mike Hunt.
> Brian: She's looking for her cunt.
>
> *Annie realises and starts to cry. Mandy takes her back to the trading booth.*
>
> Mandy: Don't worry, they do it to everyone when they're new.[53]

The language of the Stockmarket is incoherent, disintegrated, aggressively reductive and exclusive. This example shows men treating the women like any other commodity in which to trade. While throughout the play both men and women use 'cunt' to describe one another, the word never loses its sexually derogative connotation. And the last 'cunt' joke of the play, voiced by men, confirms this:

> Vince: Why's a clitoris like a filofax?
> Dave & others: Every cunt's got one.[54]

Only superficially is this a joke of solidarity against the now vulgar badge of the yuppie, it discriminates more precisely against women in the group.[55]

---

53 Caryl Churchill, *Serious Money* in *Plays: Two* (Methuen, London, 1990), pp. 248, 251.
54 Ibid., p. 302.
55 Churchill seems to share Deborah Cameron's scepticism about the possibility, entertained by some feminists (e.g. Mary Daly), of reclaiming such terms. See Cameron, op. cit. (1985), pp. 76–80. However, Churchill's insistent use of the term 'cunning woman' by female characters in *Vinegar Tom* (1976) to refer to a character later condemned as a witch, indicates that she has entertained sympathy with the feminist reclamation exercise on 'cunt'. Churchill's female characters swear much less readily than those of Andrea

Sarah Daniels, in *Masterpieces* (1983), fiercely condemns all such language and jokes as sexist and as marks on a scale of pornographic behaviour. Like *Top Girls*, this play depicts a conflict between middle and working class women, although they are not sisters and they are ultimately united by a shared battle against exploitative behaviour by men. As in the conversation between Marlene and Joyce, Daniels weights the dialogue so that the working class woman, for all her 'incorrect' grammar, dialectal and restricted vocabulary, is nevertheless shown to be the shrewder conversational tactician, more humorous and more obviously morally 'right' than her hierarchical superior. Hilary speaks in cockney, while Rowena, her social worker, speaks in an unmarked standard:

> Rowena:  Is there anything you're concerned about that I might be of help with?
> Hilary:  Money.
> Rowena:  Well, as you know we have no means of offering long term financial support.[56]

Like Marlene, when challenged, Rowena retreats into evasive administrative clichés that are designed to block further questions and which communicate no relevant information. Hilary is not put off:

> Hilary:  You have no means of offering nothing. What d'you do, eh? All the people you see, the only thing what's wrong with their lives is money and all your fancy ideas and posh words can't cover up nothing. At the end of the bleedin' day the only advice you can give us is to march in and say (*She assumes a German accent.*) 'You vill learn to budget'.[57]

The two women do speak different languages commensurate with the differing socio-economic worlds they inhabit. Hilary's military parody depicts Rowena as representative of a type that is dictatorial, aggressively invasive and male. It also reflects the fact that Hilary is aware

---

Dunbar, but this is likely to reflect both the different classes represented by their work and the fact that Churchill's work is more obviously stylised. For an account of the cultural stereotype surrounding the taboo on women swearing see Coates, op. cit. (1986), pp. 108–9.

[56] Sarah Daniels, *Masterpieces* in *Plays: One* (Methuen, London, 1991), pp. 184–5.

[57] Ibid., p. 185.

that she herself is being treated as a type, not as an individual. Hilary parodies the role of irresponsible single mother which Rowena's behaviour forces her into, but she is equally capable of stepping out of type: 'I see, now you want to prove you can't be manipulated. Yeah, big word for me ain't it?'.[58] A main source of Hilary's power is her superior linguistic playfulness, defiance which masks social impotence.

Later Rowena is interviewed against her will by a male psychiatrist who must establish whether she was insane when she pushed a man under a tube train. In these circumstances Rowena's linguistic strategies echo those which Hilary had used in self-defence. She becomes linguistically playful, sarcastic, uncooperative, stepping in and out of the roles which the psychiatrist ascribes to her, e.g.:

> Rowena: I could say, I can continuously compromise my iconoclasm with conformist clothing camouflage when complying with the correctness demanded of ceremonies such as these.
> . . .
> Psychiatrist: What I meant was, I am given to understand, that during the last few months you wore jeans constantly.
> Rowena: If you believe that's a symptom of madness, I'd keep quiet if I were you.
> Psychiatrist: And in the last six months before you left your husband, your sexual life was unsatisfactory.
> Rowena: No. We didn't do it, which was very satisfactory as far as I'm concerned.[59]

Rowena, like Hilary earlier, consistently defies Grice's 'co-operative principle' and the rules of quantity, quality, relation and manner, which he argues govern the conduct of normal conversation.[60] Like Philomele or Mary Traverse, Rowena discovers freedom from the constraints of orderly conversation when she has stepped outside the bounds of her previously ordered life. Equally, like Mary Traverse and like Hilary, Rowena only exercises this freedom in the context of a

---

58 Ibid., p. 185.
59 Ibid., pp. 207–8.
60 H.P. Grice sets out these rules in *Logic and Conversation* (1975); for a brief account of them, see Wardhaugh, op. cit. (1986), pp. 281–87. Some feminist critics (e.g. Cameron, op. cit. (1985)) object to Grice's principles, on the grounds that conversations are rarely undertaken solely with the view to exchanging information – one of his basic premises.

situation which she has politically lost, although she retains the upper moral ground. Her skilful refusal to play the interview game, reflects the fact that she knows she cannot win according to the rules invoked by those politically more powerful than herself. This kind of behaviour suggests that women of all classes can discover verbal freedom when, aware of the stereotypes into which they are cast, they step in and out of role at will. Their interlocutors (and audience, in the theatre) are thereby subjected to a kind of Brechtian alienation, to force a reassessment of the treatment of women.

The linguistic archness with which men seek to humiliate or subjugate women in the work of Churchill or Daniels does not translate to the working class context of Andrea Dunbar's work. The conflict of interest and collision of will that divide the sexes on the Bradford housing estate of *The Arbor* (1980) are expressed more blatantly, although the power balance appears at first to be less one-sided:

Girl:   You're frightened of asking, aren't you?
Boy:    Yes. Well I suppose I am. If you were me would you come straight out with it?
Girl:   Yes I would. Look I know you want it but I'm afraid it's the wrong week.[61]

The girl gives in to the sexual tension first, and helps the boy out of the behaviour socially expected of him by broaching a conversation about 'asking'. This meta-conversation, allows both of them to play up to recognised stereotype (indicated by their generic 'names') while also saving face: the girl takes control of the situation and reduces its threat, the boy does not have to suffer direct rejection.[62] But her negotiating skills desert her as the scene develops:

Girl:   I don't want to be pregnant. It's all very well for you.
Boy:    So I'll use a Durex.
Girl:   Not on me you won't.
Boy:    Why not?
Girl:   Because you won't.
Boy:    Go on. If we use one you won't get pregnant then. It's better to be safe than sorry, isn't it?

61 Andrea Dunbar, *The Arbor* in *Rita, Sue and Bob Too with The Arbor and Shirley*, introd. Rob Ritchie (Methuen, London, 1988), p. 5.
62 For an account of politeness and face-work in relation to sexual stereotyping see Coates, op. cit. (1986), pp. 109–112.

Girl:  I don't care. You're not using one of them on me.
Boy:  Go on.
Girl:  No.
Boy:  Without one then.
Girl (*pause*): OK.[63]

The boy's reasoning, pleading and clichés are not the speech acts of a confident person, but he cunningly turns the debate from whether to have sex or not, to whether to use contraception or not. The girl, as if linguistically paralysed by what seems to be the inevitable fate of the encounter, offers unadorned verbal resistance which she cannot maintain in action.

In the next scene the girl, fifteen years old, tells her family that she is pregnant, and a microcosmic picture of the way she will be bullied, oppressed and ostracised by society at large during the rest of the play is presented in the verbal storm that erupts. All participants adopt stereotypical roles: the father wishes to revenge his wronged daughter and then disowns her ('All we fuckin' want to know is who the father of it is' . . . 'She's no fuckin' daughter of mine'); the mother is keen to support her child against all odds; the sister is the first to voice public censure against the 'fuckin' slag'. Throughout the satirically astute scene the girl insists on her right to privacy and silence, observing the neglect of her needs that is masked by her father's abusive noise with 'Oh go fuck off will you'. She also defies her mother's last offer of support which is couched in terms of the verbal bullying she will get from the community – 'don't come running to me when people start calling you'.[64] As in the first scene, a bravado of assertion is used by the girl in oppressive situations. Although ostensibly at the centre of the issue, she is not less marginal to the debate than was Queen Christina. And like the monarch, the girl discovers that the isolation imposed on her by society becomes necessary for her survival.

Finally she takes refuge in a hostel, away from her home in The Arbor. The play concludes:

Girl:  It may be a dump but I quite miss it myself, funny ain't it?
Maureen:  Miss it?
Girl:  Well I miss my mum and the kids and funnily enough, I miss my dad. And all my mates. (*Pause.*) It's very quiet here.

63 *The Arbor*, pp. 5–6.
64 *The Arbor*, p. 8.

Maureen's support of her efforts to escape the housing estate, are reflected linguistically. Maureen's quizzical echo 'miss it?' elicits further articulate response from the girl, enabling her to speak her mind. It is a calming, therapeutic, non-competitive conversation between female friends,[65] and in this respect differs from virtually every other dialogue in the play.

All three of Dunbar's published plays end with women talking together, and each ending seems more positive than the last. The women, drawing strength from their own company, stop conforming to type, and recognise how language has been used as an instrument of control. *Rita, Sue and Bob Too* (1982) closes on a conversation between Michelle the deserted wife, and Sue's mother. It is an opportunity for Michelle to turn betrayal into liberation by rejecting the stereotypical role she had accepted hitherto:

> Michelle: They all try and tell you what to do. It's all right for them to do what they want. But when it comes to you, oh no, you're the wife. Stop at home, look after the kids, cook for me, that's what men want you for. And sex of course. They can't do without that can they.[66]

The word 'wife' is defined here as a number of constraining imperatives issued by 'they'. Michelle's understanding of the word in these terms reflects her new command of the situation, her rejection of the male use of 'wife', and the role it encodes. Rita and Sue, however, can be seen as victims of social gender stereotypes at the start of the play and only Sue later breaks free of them. This stereotyping is reflected in their verbal behaviour throughout the first scene, although it is complicated by the fact that they are also knowingly role-playing. Bob, Michelle's husband, thinks he is seducing the girls in his car, and he begins by asking whether they are both 'virgin'.[67] They clearly believe that it behoves them to be innocent, and having asserted this they must keep it up. And so the lesson in sex education and contraception begins, which rapidly turns into a vocabulary lesson:

> Sue: Well instead of using the proper names, use hard-on and things like that. Because that's all we understand.

---

[65] *The Arbor*, p. 42. Coates, op. cit. (1986), pp. 152–54 argues from empirical observation that these are distinguishing features of all-women conversations.
[66] *Rita, Sue and Bob Too*, p. 72.
[67] Ibid., p. 45.

Rita:   Yes you should. We've never been taught words like erection
and Durex.
. . .
Bob:    . . . And say you had sexual intercourse.
Rita (*butting in*): You mean 'have it off'?
Bob:    Yes. Well let's say if you 'have it off', the sperm will be able to
fertilise the egg.
Sue:    What do you mean exactly when you say 'the sperm'?
Bob:    It's what a man ejaculates. 'Shoots his muck' you'd say. That's
what you call 'sperm'. So it all works out that if there's a tear or a
hole in a Durex.
Sue:    Rubber-johnny.
Bob:    Rubber-johnny then . . .[68]

Sufficient guarantee of their virginity is provided by this linguistic
masquerade and Bob is willing to play them along, flattered whether
he believes them or not. The girls knowingly confuse innocence with
ignorance (both of which are feigned), in order to get what they want,
which is sex. Their linguistic foreplay establishes traditional male-
female roles of leader and led, but it is done by setting (male) standard
against (female) colloquial English. The professed inability to recognise the authoritative terms of the standard, and an insistance that
Bob should use their colloquial terms indicate, however, that the girls
are carefully inverting the traditional gender roles of seduction.

The most disempowered member of society, whether queen or call
girl, is the convict. Guilt is determined by some kind of deviation
from a social norm. In *Mary Queen of Scots* the convict's deviance is
marked by her Scottish dialect, her Catholicism, and her whoring
alter ego. These symptoms parallel those explored by Wertenbaker's
*Our Country's Good* (1988) which focuses on the life and language of
the convict. Set in the eighteenth century, it depicts a group of British
prisoners shipped to Australia where they rehearse and perform Farquhar's *The Recruiting Officer*. The title of Wertenbaker's play is taken
from the prologue of the play-within-the-play, written by one of the
male convicts: 'True patriots all; for be it understood,/ we left our
country for our country's good'.[69] The thorough ambiguity of this
prologue is a bitter example of the kind of language which, as we have
seen, Marcuse presents as typical of the dominant group in a capitalist

[68] Ibid., pp. 46–7.
[69] Timberlake Wertenbaker, *Our Country's Good* (1988; Methuen, London,
1991), p. 89.

society; these convicts can adopt the linguistic code of their op-
pressors with flair. The artificiality of the distinction between convict
and captor is exposed by the play-within-the-play, and the justice of
the players' condemnation is questioned.

However, outside this entertainment, there is little sense of equity.
Marcuse notes that in the face of a dominant language immune
against protest,

> [t]he popular language strikes with spiteful and defiant humour at
> the official and semi-official discourse. Slang and colloquial speech
> have rarely been so creative.[70]

And Wertenbaker puts the most creative vernacular into the mouth
of one female (and therefore most disempowered) convict, Liz, whose
monologue opens Act II. She and three male companions are sitting
in chains:

Liz:    Luck? Don't know the word. Shifts its bob when I comes near.
Born under a ha'penny planet I was. Dad's a nibbler, don't want to
get crapped. Mum leaves. Five brothers, I'm the only titter. I takes
in washing. Then. My own father . . . He don't want me. Liz, he
says, why trine for a make, when you can wap for a winne? I'm no
dimber mort, I says. Don't ask you to be a swell mollisher, Sister,
men want Miss Laycock, don't look at your mug . . . And you,
Wisehammer, how did you get here?

Wisehammer: Betrayal. Barbarous falsehood. Intimidation. Injus-
tice.

Liz:    Speak in English, Wisehammer.[71]

The vitality of Liz's speech is at odds with her enforced physical
passivity; having fought and lost against the ruling power she cannot
recognise even its linguistic standard as part of her own culture. As
her companion continues to protest his innocence, she replies: 'It
doesn't matter what you say. If they say you're a thief, you're a thief.'
Truth is irrelevant in this society of *Through The Looking Glass* justice.

And where justice operates in such an arbitrary fashion, the only
rational position for the accused to adopt is to keep silence. Liz makes
precisely this point on two occasions. First when she is measured for

70 Marcuse (op. cit. 1968), p. 86.
71 *Our Country's Good*, pp. 53–54.

hanging (II.6), and second when she is questioned about whether she is guilty of the crime (stealing food) for which she may be hung. Her refusal to speak is taken as a sign of guilt.[72] Eventually, however:

Phillip:  Why wouldn't you say any of this before?
. . .
Liz:  Because it wouldn't have mattered.
Phillip:  Speaking the truth?
Liz:  Speaking.[73]

Outcast and abused, silence is imposed on Liz as effectively as it was on Philomele. She is confident that she will not be believed. There is, however, reprieve for Liz: in this instance the word of a (female) convict is taken to stand against the word of a (male) soldier. With power held more evenly, Liz is free to take her part in the play and she promises with fine ambiguity 'to speak Mr Farquhar's lines with the elegance and clarity their own worth commands'.[74] Theatre, it seems, can empower women with some degree of linguistic franchise.

The abilities to command many voices and to play many parts have emerged from this survey as a survival strategies for women. Those women, ostensibly powerful, who lack linguistic versatility, such as Queen Christina or Marlene, appear dramatically weak. While those who can switch linguistic codes according to context enjoy greater power whatever their status. Related to power generated by the switching of codes, is the ability to step in and out of both behavioural and linguistic stereotype. But, as Wertenbaker's plays seem to show, only so much female transgression will be tolerated by a male hegemony before there is complete breakdown of the social order.

One area of concern exhibited in all the work considered here is the vulnerability of female characters to the power of name calling. Queen Elizabeth knows that her status is in jeopardy if enemies have the chance to call her Mrs Dudley; her anxiety is no less acute than that of the working class mother in Dunbar's Shirley (1986), who confesses to her daughter:

Mother:  Every name you can think of, I was called it.
Shirley:  Didn't it bother you?

---

72 Ibid., p. 80.                    74 Ibid., p. 83.
73 Ibid., p. 82.

Mother:   Course it did. I didn't let them see it did though or they'd of called me all the more.[75]

Whether 'Mrs', 'wife' or any other 'name you can think of', the women in these plays battle constantly against being trapped by the terms for their marital or sexual relations, or anatomised and dissected by names. Men are of course vulnerable here too, but as the example of Tereus shows, they can answer words with physical violence, and more is tolerated of them. Power is easier to keep than to take.

But the imposition of silence on Philomele works ultimately to her advantage because she is forced to find alternative means of communication which side-step the dispensation of the dominant group. Her passage of transgression offers a mythological model for the re-ordering of society. The kind of strength gained by Philomele's silence points towards the social realism of *The Arbor* where the girl (in scene two) retains a potent integrity by defying the different attempts by members of her family to make her 'tell'. Chosen silence is the most radical form of refusal to entertain the conventions of discourse, but other forms of non co-operation such as Rowena's strategies against the psychiatrist, or Liz's use of the vernacular, participate in a campaign for equity. Taken together, these playwrights challenge the ways in which linguistic folklore and sexual stereotyping are used to authorise the political status quo where powerful and uncompromised women are still a minority, and invite women to take the initiative for change.

[75] Dunbar, *Shirley*, op. cit., p. 101.

# In Defence of Celia: Discourse Analysis and Women's Discourse in 'As You Like It'

## CLARA CALVO

*'Thou art a fool; she robs thee of thy name,*
*And thou wilt show more bright and seem more virtuous*
*When she is gone'*

(*As You Like It*, I.iii.76–78)[1]

IN 1985, AN RSC PRODUCTION of *As You Like It*, with Fiona Shaw as Celia and Juliet Stevenson as Rosalind, tried to explore an aspect of this Shakespearean comedy which is often absent from dramatic productions and critical discussions of the play: the friendship between Rosalind and Celia. These two actresses have since commented on their respective experiences as the Rosalind and Celia of this production in *Clamorous Voices*,[2] a book which brings together the voices of several actresses who have struggled to liberate Shakespearean women from secular stereotypes. For Stevenson and Shaw, one of the most innovative aspects of their performance was that they found themselves forced to explore and analyse the relationship between the two cousins and friends.[3] As a result, *As You Like It* became for them a play which no longer revolved around a single heroine.

As has happened with other important aspects of an apparently uncomplicated play, the discourse of friendship which permeates the witty repartee which passes between Celia and Rosalind has not been the object of much critical attention. *As You Like It* is one of the best known plays in the Shakespearean canon: it is regularly performed in the theatre, it is frequently selected as a set text in educational institutions and it is continually discussed and reinterpreted by academic criticism. Yet despite all the attention it constantly receives, there are still aspects of the play which remain unaddressed. Apart from some

---

[1] Quotations from *As You Like It* have been taken from the New Arden edition of the play, ed. by Agnes Latham (Methuen, London, 1975).
[2] Carol Rutter, *Clamorous Voices: Shakespeare's Women Today* (The Women's Press, London, 1988).
[3] Ibid., p. 97.

recent studies,[4] the interest aroused by the figure of Rosalind has
tended to eclipse the importance of other characters and to discourage
the asking and answering of questions which are central to the play.
Peter Erickson offers an explanation for this paradoxical state of
affairs:

> Rosalind's androgynous allure can appear so attractive, her linguis-
> tic virtuosity so engaging, that all our attention becomes focused on
> her, as if nothing else happened or mattered. Her talking circles
> around Orlando seem sufficient proof of her complete triumph. Yet
> this line of response is deficient because it ignores important parts
> of the play; that is, political power is a significant element in As You
> Like It.[5]

This chapter will try to explore another significant element in the
play's polyphony – the discourse of friendship – mainly through a
study of the linguistic behaviour of one of its characters: Celia. I will
attempt to show how the discourse of friendship in As You Like It is
shaped by the use Celia makes of **positive politeness**.[6] At the same
time, I will try to show that Celia, rather than being a mere appendage and dumb companion to her cousin Rosalind, possesses her own
very personal voice. Before doing so, however, it is necessary to see
how Rosalind's presence has frequently contributed to Celia's absence
from critical appraisals of the play.

---

4  See for instance Louis Adrian Montrose ' "The place of a brother" in As
You Like It: Social Process and Comic Form', Shakespeare Quarterly, 32
(1981), 28–54 and Elaine Hobby, ' "My affection hath and unknown
bottom": Homosexuality and the teaching of As You Like It', in Lesley Aers
and Nigel Wheale, eds., Shakespeare in the Changing Curriculum (Routledge,
London, 1991), pp. 125–142.
5  Peter Erickson, 'Sexual politics and sexual structure in As You Like It', in
Harold Bloom, ed., William Shakespeare's As You Like It (Chelsea House, New
York, 1988), p. 113.
6  Penelope Brown and Stephen C. Levinson, Politeness: Some Universals in
Language Usage (Cambridge University Press, Cambridge, 1987). First pub-
lished in 1978 as 'Universals in language usage: politeness phenomena' in
E.N. Goody, ed., Questions and Politeness: Strategies in Social Interaction
(Cambridge University Press, Cambridge), pp. 56–289.

## The Rosalind myth

There is clearly no doubt about Rosalind's importance for the play as a whole; but it is also true that through performance and criticism, the centrality of Rosalind has been blown out of proportion. Thanks to a tradition of theatrical representation and theatre reviews, Rosalind has become an idealised construct: a paragon of feminine virtues, a female ideal. Academic critics – both male and female – have also contributed to foster the Rosalind myth: Rosalind has no equal, except perhaps Hamlet, and As You Like It is her play just as Hamlet is Hamlet's.[7] It is not my intention to deny Rosalind her fundamental role in the play but it seems to me that the excessive foregrounding of Rosalind has at times been achieved at the expense of ignoring Celia's contribution to the play. The centering of Rosalind partly rests on the decentering of her cousin Celia. Parallel to the emergence of the myth of Rosalind as the ideal representation of woman, there seems to have been a tendency towards the construction of a negative image for Celia. Either she has been utterly ignored, as if not relevant for the play, or her character has been assessed negatively. If mentioned at all, Celia is generally seen as an imperfect attempt at womanhood. Rosalind has to shine alone on her pedestal of perfection.

In an article entitled, 'Shakespeare's Rosalind and her public image', Mary Hamer has shown how a long established stage tradition has contributed to turn Rosalind into 'a sort of moral model or ideal'.[8] From the mid-eighteenth century onwards, the role of Rosalind in theatrical productions became set and predictable: critics and audiences shared a set of assumptions about how Rosalind should be performed. She was regarded as the repository of all feminine virtues, particularly those of tenderness, joyful charm, loveliness and sweetness. These qualities became recurrent in the assessment of the character and of the actresses who performed Rosalind. By the 1960s, the representation of Rosalind had become 'idealized in both moral and physical terms'.[9] Hamer describes the Rosalind myth as follows:

> It is a myth of femininity, in which weakness and potency are reconciled, feminine allure and mystery reassuringly garbed in

---

[7] Harold Bloom, ed., op. cit. (1988), p. 1.
[8] Mary Hamer, 'Shakespeare's Rosalind and her public image', *Theatre Research International*, 11, 2 (1986), p. 107.
[9] Ibid., p. 107.

masculine attire. This involves the metamorphosis of traditionally female vices. Talking too much and being a bit bossy are with Rosalind transformed into signs of capacity and power. It is rare to meet the suggestion that Rosalind offers a single feature to inspire criticism or even speculation of any but the most adulatory kind.[10]

Even Rosalind's loquacity is regarded as a virtue: Rosalind's prattle is seen as a projection of her joyful charm, her vitality and her energy. Rosalind's talk has been compared to birds twittering and 'overflowing with life'.[11] Also, Rosalind is suitably distanced from other witty and verbally gifted Shakespearean heroines such as Beatrice in *Much Ado About Nothing* and Katerina in *The Taming of the Shrew*. Unlike these, Rosalind '*never* talks merely for talking's sake'.[12]

The development of a stage tradition of sweet, tender and charming Rosalinds created the expectation that all Rosalinds had to conform to this feminine ideal and if an actress failed to meet these requirements, audiences and critics would be disappointed. This explains why Katherine Hepburn's 1950's Rosalind was criticised precisely for not having those qualities; in a review of Hepburn's performance, a critic writes: 'Doubtless she lacks the tenderness of Mrs. Barry, Mrs. Siddon's smile of tragedy, the naivete of Mrs. Jordan, the sweetness of Lily Langtry, and the lovely voice of Ada Rehan.'[13]

Next to this stage tradition of a sweet and lovable but also witty and energetic Rosalind there is a critical tradition which praises Rosalind above most other Shakespearean heroines for her wit and her courage. This critical tradition constantly stresses Rosalind's centrality in the play: Rosalind is right at the centre of her play, everything revolves around her. She is often regarded as a kind of female Prospero, exerting a magician's control over the other characters of the play. The centrality of Rosalind is so securely established that not many would question why Harold Bloom dedicates exclusively to Rosalind the Introduction to a volume which collects 'modern critical interpretations' of *As You Like It*. Bloom is, perhaps unconsciously, adding fuel to the Rosalind myth. For Bloom, there is no doubt about

---

10 Ibid., p. 109.
11 Ibid., p. 112.
12 Ibid., p. 112.
13 Mary Crapo Hyde, 'Katharine Hepburn's *As You Like It*', *Shakespeare Quarterly*, 1 (1950), p. 56.

'Rosalind's immense superiority to everyone else in her play'.[14] Amongst Rosalind's virtues, one can name her 'spontaneity', her 'sincerity' and 'her wisdom'[15] and 'in wit, intellect, and vision of herself she truly is Hamlet's equal'.[16]

If momentarily compared with her cousin Celia, 'Rosalind is simply superior in everything whatsoever',[17] and this explains why according to Bloom, 'All of us, men and women, like Rosalind best'.[18]

Bloom is not alone in commending Rosalind's virtues. Rosalind, whose ideas about women are little else than a tedious repetition of the kind of misogynistic generalizations on women's vices European medieval literature is brimming with, has also had the *placet* of feminist criticism. In *The Woman's Part*, C.C. Park shows no reservations when she has to praise Rosalind.[19] Even if compared to the Beatrice of *Much Ado About Nothing*, one of Shakespeare's wittier and most articulated heroines, Rosalind gets the highiest mark: 'If Beatrice is delightful, Rosalind is even better'.[20] As far as wit and energy go, 'Rosalind has no male rival'.[21] Not only that, Rosalind is 'more than witty'.[22] Park's panegyric of Rosalind is only slightly less rapturous than Bloom's:

> As You Like It is her play. . . . it is she who moves the play. She is energetic, effective, successful. . . . She has the courage to accept exile . . . Through Imogen we can appreciate the unique position of Rosalind in her play. Rosalind's decisions control the progress of As You Like It . . .[23]

Is it really Rosalind who moves the play? Sometimes decisions which are crucial for the play's progress are not taken by Rosalind. The Rosalind myth makes it difficult to remember that Rosalind does not precisely show courage when Celia suggests they leave in search of Duke Senior and that the progress of As You Like It from the Court to Arden is not controlled by Rosalind's decision but by Celia's:

[14] Bloom (op. cit., 1988), p. vii.

[15] Ibid., p. 4.          [16] Ibid., p. 1.

[17] Ibid., p. 4.          [18] Ibid., p. 1.

[19] Clara Claiborne Park, 'As we like it: How a girl can be smart and still popular', in Carolyn Ruth Swift Lenz, Gayle Greene and Carol Thomas Neely, eds., *The Woman's Part* (University of Illinois Press, Urbana, 1980), pp. 100–116.

[20] Ibid., p. 106.          [21] Ibid., p. 107.

[22] Ibid., p. 107.          [23] Ibid., p. 107.

> *Rosalind.* Why, whither shall we go?
> *Celia.* To seek my uncle in the Forest of Arden.
> *Rosalind.* Alas what danger will it be to us,
>     Maids as we are, to travel forth so far?
>     Beauty provoketh thieves sooner than gold.
> *Celia.* I'll put myself in poor and mean attire,
>     And with a kind of umber smirch my face,
>     The like do you. So shall we pass along
>     And never stir assailants.                    (I.iii.102–110)

Critics, even feminist ones, often tend to forget that a good share of the initiative, decision and capacity for action which is thought to adorn the character of Rosalind, should in fact be attributed not to Rosalind, but to her cousin Celia.

## Celia as the anti-Rosalind

In contrast to her cousin Rosalind, Celia has not received much critical attention. Despite being the one who suggests they flee to Arden when the energetic, brave, spirited Rosalind sits down to feel sorry for herself and lament over her misfortunes, she is hardly mentioned in most critical discussions of the play.[24] In a recently published monograph on *As You Like It* which has appeared in the Harvester New Critical Introductions to Shakespeare,[25] Rosalind is given five entire sections. Other characters such as Jaques, Duke Frederick, Orlando and Touchstone have at least one whole section dedicated to each of them. Instead, Celia is regarded as an appendage to her last minute acquired husband, and she is only discussed in a section entitled 'Oliver and Celia'. This is representative of a common attitude towards Celia and Celia's relationship with Rosalind in much traditional and contemporary criticism of the play. Either Celia is not mentioned at all, or only as Oliver's wife[26] and foil to Rosalind:

---

[24] See, however, the articles by Susan Carlson and Elaine Hobby which are discussed below.

[25] John Powell Ward, *As You Like It* (Harvester Wheatsheaf, London, 1992).

[26] See, for example, Harold Jenkins's justification of Celia's marriage as a 'reward' for Oliver: according to Jenkins, rather than feeling sorry for Celia, we ought to interpret her marriage as confirmation of Oliver's miraculous conversion. Harold Jenkins, '*As You Like It*', *Shakespeare Survey*, 8 (1955) p. 41.

Rosalind's feminine virtues, her energy, her wit, her *allure* (a word which tellingly appears and reappears in descriptions of Rosalind time after time) and her sly, 'feminine' way of exerting power over Orlando are enhanced if compared with a Celia who is inevitably branded as childish, impulsive, 'bodily anxious', immature and unable to grow up.

Since she has to serve as counterpoint for Rosalind, Celia's constructed image has to be negative, derogatory. Celia is often defined in opposition to Rosalind. Celia is everything Rosalind is not. Angus McIntosh[27] has explained Rosalind's and Celia's shifts in the use of the pronouns of address *you* and *thou* by resorting to two antithetically constructed images of the two cousins: Celia is impulsive and impetuous when she talks, Rosalind is always in command of herself. Celia changes from *you* to *thou* in III.ii.240 'in the mood of an impetuous child'[28] whereas Rosalind replies in III.ii.245 'in a mood of calm'.[29] For McIntosh, Celia 'is by nature impulsive and outgoing'.[30] She is also impatient and bad-tempered: when she offers Rosalind the restitution of her rights ('You know my father hath no child but I, nor none is like to have; and truly, when he dies, thou shalt be his heir') she is having 'a momentary burst of impatience'.[31] Celia's received image as girlish and childish reappears in Louis Montrose's work: when discussing this same passage, Celia is seen to be responding to Rosalind's dejection for her banished father 'with naive girlhood loyalty'.[32] One wonders why it has to be *naive girlhood* loyalty instead of *mature woman-like* loyalty. The implication behind Montrose's interpretation seems to be that there cannot be truly sincere and mature love between two adult women, therefore if Celia feels affection for Rosalind it is only because she is still a naive, immature girl, ignorant of what being a grown-up person is like.

Celia becomes Rosalind's foil particularly when it comes to discussing their linguistic abilities. Although Celia is, as Park reminds us, the only character able to match Rosalind's repartee,[33] she still has to be antithetically placed with regard to Rosalind, so that Rosalind can be Celia's superior in everything. If Celia displays some wit, Rosalind is by far the wittier of the two: Rosalind's wit is opposed to 'Celia's wry

[27] Angus McIntosh, '*As You Like It*: a grammatical clue to character', *A Review of English Literature*, 4, 2 (1963), 68–81.
[28] Ibid., p. 77.                     [29] Ibid., p. 77.
[30] Ibid., p. 72.                     [31] Ibid., p. 73.
[32] Montrose, op. cit. (1980), p. 31.    [33] Park, op. cit. (1980), p. 107

humour'[34] and while Rosalind's 'curving flights of language grow, Celia is contrastingly terse and monotone'.[35] In fact, the language Ward uses to describe Celia's and Rosalind's talking is in itself extremely telling:

> The modes of talk in the play are many. There are gentle and harsh exchanges. There are long speeches as with Jaques most of the time, and shorter snatches . . . There are the elongating wistful curves by Rosalind where words multiply, and sharper comments from her companion Celia, who bangs home the same term sardonically five times as though she has had enough of it[36]

The rhetorical figure of parallelism which Ward is using here helps to foreground that, in case there were any doubts, Rosalind's talk is associated with 'gentle' and 'long speeches' ('elongating wistful curves') whereas the way in which Celia's talk is described inevitably echoes those 'harsh', 'shorter snatches' ('sharper comments', 'bangs', 'sardonically').

## Clamorous voices

The centrality of Rosalind and the marginality of Celia in critical appraisals of the play can be toned down with the clamorous voices of the two actresses who played these roles in Adrian Noble's 1985 production and with two critical studies by Susan Carlson and Elaine Hobby who have taken the unusual step of analysing the relationship between Rosalind and Celia.[37]

When Adrian Noble's 1985 production of As You Like It was still in the making, the friendship between Celia and Rosalind emerged as one of the issues which Juliet Stevenson, the actress playing Rosalind, considered worth exploring: 'I got snatches of a wonderful relationship between two women, Celia and Rosalind. There's no real parallel

---

[34] Edward I. Berry, 'Rosalynde and Rosalind', Shakespeare Quarterly, 31 (1980), p. 48.
[35] Ward, op. cit. (1992), p. 74.
[36] Ibid., p. 13.
[37] Susan Carlson, 'Women in As You Like It: Community, Change, and Choice', Essays in Literature, 14, 2 (1987), 151–169 and Hobby, op. cit. (1991), pp. 125–142.

to their journey anywhere in Shakespeare. I had never seen this friendship fully explored.'[38]

By foregrounding the importance of the friendship which exists between Celia and Rosalind, Fiona Shaw and Juliet Stevenson challenged one of the received images of the play: the play no longer was exclusively about Rosalind. For them, there is a balance in the roles of Celia and Rosalind. Both are central to the fabric of As You Like It, but each of them is central to well-defined, and very different, parts of the play. Celia is the one who takes the initiative and makes decisions in the first part of the play, when they are still at Court. Rosalind, who has been a mere onlooker at Court, will become the initiator once they set off for Arden. In this shift of initiative, Fiona Shaw sees 'a tension between Celia and Rosalind that challenges the actresses who play the roles.'[39]

In Act I, As You Like It still looks like a play which is going to be about Celia: she conducts the word games, she manages to cheer up Rosalind, she decides they will watch the wrestling, and she is the first to entreat Orlando not to fight. Also, it is she who suggests that they escape to Arden. However, once they start their journey, Celia's centrality to the play comes to an end. Rosalind takes over: she stops being an observer, a mere spectator as she was at Court, and becomes the centre of the action. This shift of importance means that 'Actresses who play the roles have to negotiate room for each other'.[40] Aware of this shifting of centrality and importance, Juliet Stevenson and Fiona Shaw reached an agreement. Stevenson relinquished the beginning of the play to Shaw, so that the first part of the play would be run by Celia. Meanwhile, Stevenson would play a reticent Rosalind and remain silent. Fiona Shaw agreed with her and comments: 'I in turn felt that Celia needed the focus in the first part in order to render up with grace the second half. Juliet and I became friends. The only way to do this play was to do it together.'[41]

Stevenson and Shaw's ideas about the play are surprisingly similar to those of two female critics. For Elaine Hobby, Rosalind's 'most important relationship is with her cousin, Celia'[42] and she also sees an evolution in Rosalind's and Celia's respective centrality in the play:

[38] Rutter, op. cit. (1988), p. 97.
[39] Ibid., p. 103.
[40] Ibid., p. 103.
[41] Ibid., p. 103.
[42] Hobby, op. cit. (1991), pp. 134–135.

In the initial stages of the play it is Celia, not Rosalind, who is in charge in their relationship. In I.3, Celia tries to defend Rosalind against Duke Frederick's wrath, and when that fails it is she who plans their escape from the palace. The first act is closed with Celia's words. Once Rosalind is dressed as a man, however, it seems her prediction that assuming 'a swashing and a martial outside' (I.3.118) will change her is true. When the two cousins reappear (II.4) it is Celia who begs for rest – 'I can go no further' – and Rosalind/Ganymede who boldly asserts 'I must comfort the weaker vessel, as doublet and hose ought to show itself courageous to petticoat.'[43]

Susan Carlson also sees that 'the most steady love of the play' is 'that between two women, Rosalind and Celia'[44] and that 'the cousins are inseparable until the very end of the play'.[45] Carlson notices how 'When we first meet Celia and Rosalind in I.ii, we are immediately struck by the chasm between the love, trust, and warmth of their woman's world and the harsh world depicted in I.i.'[46] She also notes that 'The third scene stands as the climax of the play's celebration of women's love. Significantly, the voice of the achievement is Celia, not Rosalind.'[47] However, unlike Stevenson, Shaw and Hobby, Carlson thinks that the turningpoint, the moment in which a change in Celia's relationship with Rosalind takes place, is not when they leave the Court and arrive in Arden with Rosalind dressed as a man. For Carlson, the moment in which Rosalind finally takes over Celia and Celia is silenced is when Ganymede begins to court Orlando: 'Yet as soon as Rosalind begins to woo Orlando, Celia falls silent.'[48]

Celia's silence in the second half of the play is a symmetrical counterpart to Rosalind's laconic disposition in Act I.[49] Celia's silence is, however, much more noticeable than Rosalind's, perhaps because, although Celia is always present at Rosalind's wooing games with Orlando, she hardly ever utters a word. She only addresses Orlando and Rosalind once, when she has been asked to serve as priest and marry them. Celia's silent presence at the wooing games has been

43 Ibid., p. 135.                    44 Carlson, op. cit. (1987), p. 151.
45 Ibid., p. 162.                    46 Ibid., p. 160.
47 Ibid., p. 160.                    48 Ibid., p. 161.
49 Celia remarks on Rosalind's silence in I.iii.12: 'Why cousin, why Rosalind! Cupid have mercy, not a word?', and in I.iii.73–74 Duke Frederick comments on Rosalind's silence which moves people to pity her.

taken to indicate 'the disintegration of a friendship'.[50] However, before her silence becomes noticeable, Celia has shown that she can be a lively, intelligent, and extremely successful conversationalist.

## Celia as conversationalist

In her conversations with other characters, Celia behaves in a way which, from a linguistically-oriented point of view, is far from childish or naive. She has at her command a good set of linguistic abilities which enable her to perform a wide range of linguistic functions: she can be deferential to her father in I.iii.62 or in I.iii.81–82; in I.iii.68–72, she can eloquently defend Rosalind, who has been accused of treason by Duke Frederick. She can even contradict and correct her father's inexactitudes without being disrespectful:

> Duke Frederick.  Ay Celia, we stay'd her for your sake,
>      Else had she [Rosalind] with her father rang'd along.
> Celia.  I did not then entreat to have her stay;
>      It was your pleasure and your own remorse.     (I.iii.63–66)

Celia can also rebuke her father's fool, Touchstone, for his excessive familiarity in I.iii.77–79 and ridicule a silly courtier in I.iii.86–137. However, it is in her conversations with Rosalind that Celia most obviously displays her abilities as trained conversationalist: she can successfully entreat Rosalind to be merry in I.ii; persuade her to flee to Arden in I.iii; tease her and make fun of her in III.iv and take her to task for her unnatural remarks on women in IV.i.

Celia and Rosalind have several opportunities during the play to engage in conversation in private. There are in fact seven of these occasions: three of them occur in Act I, before they leave the Court for Arden (I.ii.1–53; I.iii.1–36 and I.iii.86–134) and the other four in Acts III and IV, once they are already in the forest (III.ii.160–248; III.iv.1–42; IV.i.191–207 and IV.iii.1–15). It is worth noticing that the three duologues the two cousins have in Act I are opened and closed by Celia, not Rosalind. This indicates that when the two cousins are together, Celia talks more than Rosalind. Celia has in these 3 duologues a total of 26 conversational turns, 3 more than Rosalind, who has only 23 turns. In Arden, both cousins have a

---

similar number of turns – Celia has 34 and Rosalind 33 – and Celia's control over the boundaries of the duologues is not so spectacular: of these other four interactions, Rosalind opens two (III.iv.1 and IV.iii.1) and closes one (III.ii.248); Celia opens two (III.ii.160 and IV.i.191) and closes three (III.iv.42; IV.i.207 and IV.iii.5) but she only both opens and closes one duologue (IV.i.191–207).

Celia's opening and closing of the cousins' three duologues in Act I suggest that she enjoys a greater degree of control over the topic(s) of conversation than her friend Rosalind. At least she has more opportunities of introducing conversational topics than Rosalind. A participant in a conversation usually has the possibility of introducing a new conversational topic with each new conversational turn. In this sense, the first turn in an interaction is always a privileged slot: the speaker has no topic constraints and the introduction of a topic which in other slots is optional is here obligatory. So in these seven duologues between the two cousins, Celia, having a total of four conversational turns more than Rosalind, has more opportunities than Rosalind to control the topic of conversation; also, since she has five first-turn-in-the-interaction oportunities in contrast to Rosalind's two, she enjoys a greater number of topic-introduction slots. So when the two cousins and friends are together, Celia's role as conversationalist is not at all obscured by Rosalind's presence.

In her conversations with Rosalind, Celia often makes use of a series of sophisticated linguistic strategies in order to achieve her conversational goals. Sometimes, for instance, she can manipulate the development of the talk in order to introduce the conversational topics which suit her. In I.iii.22–26, Celia puts a stop to her jesting with Rosalind because she wants to discuss a serious topic with her cousin: Rosalind's sudden infatuation with Orlando. Celia's conversational expertise enables her to ensure that the shift of topic is smooth. She does not introduce the new topic abruptly at the beginning of her turn; instead, she replies to Rosalind's previous turn and only when that is done does she venture to introduce the new topic:

> Celia.  Come, come, wrestle with thy affections.
> Rosalind.  O they take the part of a better wrestler than myself.
> Celia.  O a good wish upon you! You will cry in time, in despite of a fall. But turning these jests out of service, let us talk in good earnest. Is it possible, on such a sudden, you should fall into so strong a liking with old Sir Rowland's youngest son?                                        (I.iii.20–26)

With the help of discourse analysis[51] it is possible to see that here Celia achieves her smooth change of topic because she produces, in the same conversational turn, two moves. The first move in the turn is a FOLLOW-UP or FEEDBACK, which forms part of a three-move exchange:

INITIATION   Celia.   Come, come, wrestle with thy affections.
RESPONSE   Rosalind.   O they take the part of a better wrestler than myself.
FOLLOW-UP   Celia.   O a good wish upon you! You will cry in time, in despite of a fall.

The second move in the turn is a new INITIATION, the first move of a new exchange and the move which introduces the change of topic:

INITIATION   Celia.   . . . But turning these jests out of service, let us talk in good earnest. Is it possible, on such a sudden, you should fall into so strong a liking with old Sir Rowland's youngest son?

Celia continues to use this conversational strategy for the rest of the scene and with its help she exerts an obvious control over the topical development of the talk:

INITIATION   Celia.   . . . But turning these jests out of service, let us talk in good earnest. Is it possible, on such a sudden, you should fall into so strong a liking with old Sir Rowland's youngest son?
RESPONSE   Rosalind.   The Duke my father loved his father dearly.
FOLLOW-UP   Celia.   Doth it therefore ensue that you should love his son dearly?

INITIATION   Celia.   By this kind of chase, I should hate him, for my father hated his father dearly; yet I hate not Orlando.
RESPONSE   Rosalind.   No faith, hate him not, for my sake.
FOLLOW-UP   Celia.   Why should I not?

INITIATION   Celia.   Doth he not deserve well?

---

[51] John McH. Sinclair and R.M. Coulthard, *Towards an Analysis of Discourse: The English Used by Teacher and Pupils* (Oxford University Press, London, 1975).

RESPONSE  *Rosalind.* Let me love him for that, and do you love
            him because I do.    (I.iii.23–35)

In this scene, Celia produces mostly INITIATION and FOLLOW-UP
moves, the moves which in classroom discourse are the prerogative of
teachers. Rosalind, instead, produces nothing but RESPONSE moves,
the moves pupils are expected to produce. With this, it is not my
intention to suggest that the relationship between Celia and her
cousin Rosalind is shaped by the same power relation which generally
obtains between teachers and their pupils. Celia does not enjoy the
role features which, as Margaret Berry has shown,[52] are normally
enjoyed by a teacher: [+ HIGHER] and [+ PRIMARY KNOWER]. It is not
possible to predict then that when Rosalind and Celia talk in private,
Celia will always have the INITIATIONS and FOLLOW-UPS. However,
the parallelism between the moves teachers use in a classroom and the
moves Celia produces in this scene shows that sometimes Celia exerts
a great deal of control over the topic of the conversation, in this case
by means of the sustained use of an apparently simple but very effective conversational strategy.

In III.ii, when the two cousins have just found Orlando's poems in
praise of Rosalind hanging from the trees of Arden, Celia displays
another of her conversational strategies: she artfully slows down the
pace of the talk in order to tease Rosalind. She achieves this aim by
deliberately witholding information and her conversational strategy is
to produce a move which resembles a FOLLOW-UP rather than a
RESPONSE when the predicted and expected move is a RESPONSE:

INITIATION  *Rosalind.*  Is it a man?
RESPONSE    *Celia.*  And a chain, that you once wore, about his
              neck.

INITIATION  *Celia.*  Change you colour?

INITIATION  *Rosalind.*  I prithee who?
FOLLOW-UP   *Celia.*  O Lord, Lord! It is a hard matter for friends to
              meet; but mountains may be remov'd with
              earthquakes, and so encounter.

[52] Margaret Berry, 'Is teacher an unanalysed concept?', in M.A.K. Halliday
and Robin P. Fawcett, eds., *New Developments in Systemic Linguistics, Volume
1: Theory and Description* (Pinter, London, 1987), pp. 41–63.

INITIATION   *Rosalind.* Nay, I prithee now, with most petitionary
            vehemence, tell me who it is.
FOLLOW-UP   *Celia.* O wonderful, wonderful! and most wonderful
            wonderful! And yet again wonderful! And after that
            out of all whooping.
INITIATION   *Rosalind.* Good my complexion! Dost thou think
            though I am caparisoned like a man I have a doublet
            and hose in my disposition? One inch of delay more
            is a South Sea of discovery. I prithee tell me who is it
            quickly, and speak apace. I would thou couldst
            stammer, that thou mightst pour this concealed man
            out of thy mouth, as wine comes out of a
            narrow-mouthed bottle; either too much at once or
            none at all. I prithee take the cork out of thy mouth,
            that I may drink thy tidings.
FOLLOW-UP   *Celia.* So you may put a man in your belly.
                                                    (III.ii.177–201)

Later on in the same scene (III.ii), Celia shows that she knows how
to make use of one of the conventions of the locally managed system
of turn-taking:[53] the right to enjoy an extended conversational turn,
the right not to be interrupted while she delivers the information
Rosalind has requested of her. According to the rules of turn-taking,
speakers can easily lose the floor at every TRANSITION RELEVANCE
PLACE,[54] 'unless permission has been sought for a longer turn, perhaps
to tell a story or a joke'.[55] The exploitation of the rules of turn-taking
on Celia's part – her insistence in claiming her extended turn – helps
to bring to the fore Rosalind's 'impatient', 'childish' behaviour:

> *Rosalind.* Alas the day, what shall I do with my doublet and
> hose? What did he when thou saw'st him? What said he?
> How looked he? Wherein went he? What makes he here?
> Did he ask for me? Where remains he? How parted he with
> thee? And when shalt thou see him again? Answer me in
> one word.

---

[53] Harvey Sacks, Emanuel A. Schegloff and Gail Jefferson, 'A simplest syste-
matics for the organization of turntaking for conversation', *Language*, 50, 4
(1974), 696–735.
[54] Ibid., p. 703.
[55] Malcolm Coulthard, *An Introduction to Discourse Analysis*, second edition
(Longman, London, 1985), p. 61.

*Celia.* You must borrow me Gargantua's mouth first. 'Tis a word too great for any mouth of this age's size. To say ay and no to these particulars is more than to answer in a catechism.

*Rosalind.* But doth he know that I am in this forest, and in man's apparel? Looks he as freshly as he did the day he wrestled?

*Celia.* It is as easy to count atomies as to resolve the propositions of a lover. But take a taste of my finding him, and relish it with good observance. I found him under a tree like a dropped acorn.

*Rosalind.* It may well be called Jove's tree, when it drops such fruit.

*Celia.* Give me audience, good madam.

*Rosalind.* Proceed.

*Celia.* There lay he stretched along like a wounded knight.

*Rosalind.* Though it be pity to see such a sight, it well becomes the ground.

*Celia.* Cry holla to the tongue, I prithee; it curvets unseasonably. He was furnished like a hunter.

*Rosalind.* O ominous! he comes to kill my heart!

*Celia.* I would sing my song without a burden. Thou bringest me out of tune.

*Rosalind.* Do you not know I am a woman? When I think, I must speak. Sweet, say on.

*Celia.* You bring me out. Soft! comes he not here?

(III.ii.215–247)

As the experienced conversationalist she is, Celia knows that she is going to need an extended conversational turn to answer Rosalind's questions about Orlando. She therefore negotiates this extended turn: 'But take a taste of my finding him, and relish it with good observance'. Rosalind, disregarding the rules of turn-taking, interrupts Celia several times with comments which protract the development of the narrative. Celia tries to make Rosalind realise the irrationality of her conversational behaviour: the incongruity of demanding information and then not allowing the information to be imparted. In practically every new turn of hers, Celia reminds Rosalind of her right to have an extended conversational turn: 'Give me audience, good madam'; 'Cry holla to the tongue, I prithee'; 'I would sing my song without a burden'; 'You bring me out'. Celia's function in this passage is to reveal Rosalind's uncollaborative conversational behaviour: her impatience, her irrationality and the topical-irrelevance of her comments

('O ominous! he comes to kill my heart!') are among the conventions of pastoral love. Another example of how Celia's expert conversational knowledge helps to ridicule Rosalind's stereotyped behaviour in her arcadic infatuation with Orlando can be found in III.iv.142. In this scene, Celia helps to show Rosalind's inconsistent reasoning by means of an obvious conversational technique: she produces a preferred second part for every first part of each ADJACENCY PAIR[56] initiated by Rosalind, regardless of the truth content of the proposition contained in Rosalind's first part. Thus, the contradictions in Rosalind's discourse become evident and Celia's determination to humour her cousin and avoid disagreement turn Rosalind into a comic figure.

## Positive politeness and the discourse of friendship

Celia, as it has been shown, has at her command several conversational strategies which assist her in achieving her conversational goals. One of the stategies she most often resorts to is the use of POSITIVE POLITENESS:

> Positive politeness is redress directed to the addressee's positive face, his perennial desire that his wants (or the actions/acquisitions/ values resulting from them) should be thought of as desirable. Redress consists in partially satisfying that desire by communicating that one's own wants (or some of them) are in some respects similar to the addressee's wants.[57]

The use of positive politeness indicates that the speaker wants at least some of the hearer's wants and that the speaker considers that both speaker and hearer are 'the same', belong to the same group, have the same rights and duties and can entertain expectations of reciprocity. Positive politeness brings together several linguistic strategies which show that there exists intimacy and minimal social distance between addresser and addressee. For this reason, as Brown and Levinson have observed, positive politeness strategies are not only used to repair some damage done to the addressee's face, the

---

56 Emanuel A. Schegloff and Harvey Sacks 'Opening up closings', *Semiotica*, 7, 4 (1973), 289–327.
57 Brown and Levinson, op. cit. (1987), p. 101.

hearer's self-image, but also 'as a kind of social accelerator, where S, in using them, indicates that he wants to 'come closer' to H'.[58]

It is hardly surprising then that when Celia wants to emphasize the bond of friendship which exists between her cousin and herself, she makes consistent use of most of the 15 strategies of positive politeness listed by Brown and Levinson. At the beginning of I.ii., for example, Rosalind is sad and despondent, pining for her banished father and not very inclined to engage in verbal games with Celia. Celia, instead, is determined to raise Rosalind's spirits and she manages to achieve this conversational goal with a complex battery of positive politeness strategies:

> *Celia.*   I pray thee Rosalind, sweet my coz, be merry.
> *Rosalind.*   Dear Celia, I show more mirth than I am mistress of, and would you yet I were merrier? Unless you could teach me to forget a banished father, you must not learn me how to remember any extraordinary pleasure.
> *Celia.*   Herein I see thou lov'st me not with the full weight that I love thee. If my uncle thy banished father had banished thy uncle the Duke my father, so thou hadst been still with me, I could have taught my love to take thy father for mine; so wouldst thou, if the truth of thy love to me were so righteously tempered as mine is to thee.
> *Rosalind.*   Well, I will forget the condition of my estate, to rejoice in yours.
> *Celia.*   You know my father hath no child but I, nor none is like to have; and truly when he dies, thou shalt be his heir; for what he hath taken away from thy father perforce, I will render thee again in affection. By mine honour I will, and when I break that oath, let me turn monster. Therefore my sweet Rose, my dear Rose, be merry.
> *Rosalind.*   From henceforth I will, coz, and devise sports. Let me see, what think you of falling in love?        (I.ii.1–24)

This is the first conversation the cousins have on stage and it begins with Celia producing an FTA (face-threatening act), a speech act which puts a threat to the addressee's face: Celia's first utterance in the play is a DIRECTIVE, an order expressed through an imperative ('be

---

58 Ibid., p. 103. S and H stand respectively for *Speaker* and *Hearer*. For the following analysis of Celia's use of positive politeness strategies, I have closely followed the section on positive politeness in Brown and Levinson, pp. 101–129.

merry') and as such it threatens Rosalind's right to self-preservation and to have her territory respected by others. Celia is telling Rosalind what she ought to do and this constitutes a threat to Rosalind's NEGATIVE FACE, her want not to be imposed upon. Celia nevertheless minimizes the impact of this threat with the help of several positive politeness strategies. Celia is assuming here that Rosalind wants to be merry and will cooperate to achieve this end, which is in their mutual interest (Strategy 11: *Be optimistic*). Celia, in fact, wants Rosalind to be merry as well and by expressing this wish in such a way that assumes that Rosalind wants to be merry too, Celia is putting pressure on Rosalind to cooperate with her own wants. At the same time, by wanting something that is good for Rosalind, Celia shows that she notices Rosalind's wants, that she attends to Rosalind's needs: Celia cares for her cousin and has noticed that Rosalind is not merry (Strategy 1: *Notice, attend to H's interests, needs, wants, goods*). Together with these two strategies, Celia is making use of a third one (Strategy 4: *Use in-group identity markers*) because she is addressing Rosalind with 'sweet my coz' and the pronoun of address *thou*[59] ('I pray thee'), two markers of in-group membership. With this strategy, Celia is claiming the existence of some 'common ground' between Rosalind and herself; she is also indicating that she disregards the slight difference in social status existing between them (Celia is heir to the dukedom; Rosalind has lost her former privileged position as the ruling duke's daughter) and that she considers herself Rosalind's equal.[60]

Celia's second speech in this scene also displays a cluster of positive politeness strategies. In this speech, the FTA is a complaint ('I see thou lov'st me not') which threatens Rosalind's negative face. Celia again resorts to Strategy 4: *Use in-group identity markers* and addresses Rosalind throughout the speech with the pronoun *thou*. She also makes use of Strategy 2: *Exaggerate (interest, approval, sympathy with*

<hr>

[59] As I have suggested and discussed at length in Clara Calvo, 'Pronouns of address and social negotiation in *As You Like It*', *Language and Literature*, 1, 1 (1992) 5–27, the pronoun *thou* together with its morphological variants can be considered to be often used, at least in this play if not in 16th century English, as an in-group identity marker.

[60] Brown and Levinson have noted that the combination of imperative ('pray', 'be merry') with in-group identity markers ('coz', 'thee') can turn a command into a request, because it 'indicates that S considers the relative P (power, status difference) between himself and the addressee to be small, thus softening the imperative by indicating that it isn't a powerbacked command.' Brown and Levinson, op. cit. (1987), p. 108.

H) when she describes the scope of her love for Rosalind: 'with the full weight that I love thee'; 'so righteously tempered as mine is to thee'. She is also using Strategy 2 when she claims that had her uncle banished her father her love for Rosalind would have made her take her uncle as father: 'If my uncle thy banished father had banished thy uncle the Duke my father, so thou hadst been still with me, I could have taught my love to take thy father for mine'. Here Celia is simultaneously making use of another positive politeness strategy, Strategy 13: *Give (or ask) for reasons*. Celia is giving Rosalind the reason why she claims that Rosalind does not love her: because she has not learnt to take Celia's father as her own father. As Brown and Levinson have noted, 'giving reasons is a way of implying 'I can help you' or 'you can help me' and assuming cooperation, a way of showing what help is needed'.[61] When she gives the reason why she thinks Rosalind doesn't correspond to her love, Celia is suggesting what course of action Rosalind has to follow in order to show she loves Celia as much as she is loved by her. Finally, in her second speech, Celia also makes use of Strategy 7: *Presuppose/raise/assert common ground*: 'so wouldst thou, if the truth of thy love to me were so righteously tempered as mine is to thee.' Here Celia is manipulating presupposition: she is presupposing knowledge of H's wants and attitudes.[62] Celia is presupposing that if Rosalind really loved her, Rosalind would behave as she has just described she would if she were in Rosalind's situation.

In her third speech in this scene, Celia produces several FTAs which threaten Rosalind's negative face. She first of all threatens Rosalind's negative face with an offer: 'thou shalt be his heir; for what he hath taken away from thy father perforce, I will render thee again in affection'. With this offer, Celia is putting pressure on Rosalind to accept the offer, so her negative face is threatened; and if Rosalind does accept, her negative face is also threatened because she will incur a debt.[63] Then Celia threatens Rosalind's negative face again with a promise: 'By mine honour I will, and when I break that oath, let me turn monster' and finally, she threatens Rosalind's negative face once more with a request: 'be merry', since she imposes her wants on Rosalind's freedom of action and freedom from imposition. These three FTAs are all minimised with redressive action towards

61 Ibid., p. 128.              63 Ibid., p. 66.
62 Ibid., p. 122.

Rosalind's positive face. Celia is imposing on Rosalind's right of self-preservation but she is at the same time showing that she likes and cares for Rosalind.

Throughout this third speech, Celia continues to use positive politeness strategies. She first of all uses Strategy 7: *Presuppose/raise/assert common ground*, when she asserts Rosalind's knowledge: 'You know my father hath no child but I, nor none is like to have'. By claiming this common ground, Celia is paving the way for her face-threatening offer. She also tones down this offer with Strategy 13: *Give (or ask) for reasons* when she considers her offer as the result of her affection for Rosalind: 'for what he hath taken away from thy father perforce, I will render thee again in affection'. Celia is also indicating that she has expectations of reciprocity on Rosalind's part (Strategy 14: *Assume or assert reciprocity*) when she requests that Rosalind be merry in exchange of the promise of returning the dukedom to her after Duke Frederick's death. Finally, Celia is also making use of Strategy 4: *Use in-group identity markers* ('thou', 'my sweet Rose', 'my dear Rose') and Strategy 15: *Give gifts to H*, when she makes her offer. The use of Strategy 15 manifests the speaker's choice of redressing the hearer's face by means of giving the hearer some of his or her wants. The speaker thus shows that he or she wants for the hearer what the hearer wants for himself or herself. Celia achieves success for her conversational goal to raise Rosalind's spirits with this strategy in particular: once she has promised Rosalind the inheritance of the dukedom, Rosalind gives in and begins to 'devise sports'.[64]

In I.iii., before Rosalind is banished, Celia again makes use of positive politeness strategies when she uses in-group identity markers (Strategy 4): 'Why cousin, why Rosalind' (I.iii.12) and when she cracks a joke: 'No, thy words are too precious to be cast away upon curs. Throw some of them at me; come lame me with reasons' (I.iii.4–6). She also makes use of Strategy 1: *Notice, attend to H* and Strategy

---

[64] It would not be too far-fetched to read Rosalind's sadness for her banished father as partly filial affection and partly woeful sorrow for a lost inheritance. As Louis Montrose and Peter Erickson have suggested, *As You Like It* is not only a play about youthful love: it is a play about political issues, such as inheriting property. Even the purest, soundest, apparently most disinterested love in the play, the love between Rosalind and Celia, is tainted by material interests. Rosalind forgets her banished father as soon as she has Celia's promise of restoring her to her rights. This may be an unusual, unkind reading of Rosalind's character, but a plausible one.

13: *Give (or ask) for reasons* when she enquires: 'But is all this for your father?' (I.iii.10).

In I.iii.86–103, once Rosalind has been banished by her uncle, Celia's discourse of friendship is, even more than before, cloaked in positive politeness strategies:

> *Celia.*    O my poor Rosalind, whither wilt thou go?
> Wilt thou change fathers? I will give thee mine.
> I charge thee be not thou more griev'd than I am.
> *Rosalind.*    I have more cause.
> *Celia.*    Thou hast not, cousin.
> Prithee be cheerful. Know'st thou not the Duke
> Hath banish'd me his daughter?
> *Rosalind.*    That he hath not.
> *Celia.*    No, hath not? Rosalind lacks then the love
> Which teacheth thee that thou and I am one.
> Shall we be sunder'd? Shall we part, sweet girl?
> No, let my father seek another heir.
> Therefore devise with me how we may fly,
> Whither to go and what to bear with us,
> And do not seek to take your change upon you,
> To bear your griefs yourself and leave me out.
> For by this heaven, now at our sorrows pale,
> Say what thou canst, I'll go along with thee.
> *Rosalind.*    Why, whither shall we go?
> *Celia.*    To seek my uncle in the Forest of Arden.
>
> (I.i ii.86–103)

Celia begins with an in-group identity marker ('my poor Rosalind') and consistently addresses her cousin with *thou* (Strategy 4). Then, she manifests the extent of her grief for Rosalind's banishment by saying that her own grief is greater than her cousin's: 'I charge thee be not thou more griev'd than I am' (Strategy 2: *Exaggerate interest, approval, sympathy with H*). In her second speech, Celia threatens Rosalind's face with a request: 'Prithee be cheerful'; but she softens this threat with two positive politenes strategies: 'Know'st thou not the Duke/ Hath banish'd me his daughter?' (Strategy 12: *Include both S and H in the activity* and Strategy 9: *Assert or presuppose S's knowledge of and concern for H's wants*). In her third speech, Celia makes use of Strategy 2 again to express the scope of her affection for Rosalind: 'thou and I am one', and she presupposes that none of them wants to part with each other (Strategy 7: *Presuppose common ground*): 'Shall we be sunder'd? Shall we part, sweet girl?/ No, let my father seek another heir'. Celia also uses Strategy 12: *Include both S and H in the activity* again: 'Therefore devise with me how we may fly,/ Whither to go and what to bear with us' and Strategy 1: *Notice, attend to H*: 'And do not seek to take your change upon you,/ To bear your griefs yourself and leave me out'; here Celia is also making use of Strategy 13: *Give gifts to H (sympathy, cooperation)*. Celia ends this speech with a promise to go with Rosalind (Strategy 10: *Offer, promise*): 'For by this heaven, now at our sorrows pale,/ Say what thou canst, I'll go along with thee.' With this promise, Celia is assuming that Rosalind wants her as company in her banishment (Strategy 11: *Be optimistic*).

While the two cousins are at the Court, Celia's talk is brimming with positive politeness strategies, but as soon as they arrive in Arden and they find Orlando's poems in praise of Rosalind, Celia's discourse of friendship melts, and with it her use of positive politeness. In III.ii. Celia may use the occasional in-group identity marker but there is no asserting or presupposing common ground, no stressing that Rosalind and herself are cooperators, no interest in showing that Celia wants what Rosalind wants. This is reflected in a change of politeness strategies: positive politeness is replaced by NEGATIVE POLITENESS and OFF-RECORD STRATEGIES.[65] Celia makes use of negative politeness Strategy 5: *Give deference* in III.ii.234: 'Give me audience, good madam'. 'Good madam' sharply contrasts with previous in-group identity markers: Rosalind is no longer addressed as 'sweet my coz' or 'dear Rose'. Celia also makes use of off-record Strategy 9: *Use metaphors* when she asks Rosalind to keep quiet: 'Cry holla to the tongue, I prithee, it curvets unseasonably' (III.ii.240–241) and 'I would sing my song without a burden. Thou bringest me out of tune' (III.ii.243–244). Apart from the pronoun *thou*, there is no positive politeness strategy being used by Celia here: the damage caused to Rosalind's face by Celia's FTAs is not minimised with redress for her positive face. In fact, in Arden, it is Rosalind who needs to resort to positive politeness strategies when she is rebuked by Celia for her unnatural remarks on women. In IV.i., Rosalind uses Strategy 4: *Use in-group identity markers* and Strategy 13: *Give (or ask) for reasons* in order to justify her actions:

[65] Brown and Levinson, op. cit. (1987), pp. 68–71.

> *Celia.* You have simply misused our sex in your loveprate. We must have your doublet and hose plucked over your head, and show the world what the bird hath done to her own nest.
>
> *Rosalind.* O coz, coz, coz, my pretty little coz, that thou didst know how many fathom deep I am in love! But it cannot be sounded. My affection hath an unknown bottom, like the Bay of Portugal.
>
> *Celia.* Or rather bottomless, that as fast as you pour affection in, it runs out.
>
> *Rosalind.* No. That same wicked bastard of Venus, that was begot of thought, conceived of spleen and born of madness, that blind rascally boy that abuses everyone's eyes because his own are out, let him be judge how deep I am in love. I'll tell thee Aliena, I cannot be out of the sight of Orlando. I'll go find a shadow and sigh till he come.
>
> *Celia.* And I'll sleep.                                    (IV.i.191–207)

Rosalind is here claiming common ground, reminding Celia of their bond of friendship in an attempt to appease Celia, and she constructs the discourse of friendship as Celia did in I.ii and I.iii, with the help of positive politeness strategies. Celia, instead, does not even use a single *thou* to Rosalind in this scene. The discourse of friendship has completely disappeared here from Celia's conversation with Rosalind.

## The place of a cousin in 'As You Like It'

The disappearance of positive politeness and the discourse of friend-ship from Celia's speeches in IV.i. has the function of reminding us of something which the powerful presence of the Rosalind myth often helps us to forget: that Rosalind has misused her own sex simply for the sake of her 'love-prate'. This is one of the dark sides to Rosalind's character which are usually ignored in order to magnify her virtues. Celia's place in *As You Like It* may be no more than the place of a cousin, of a disposable companion to Rosalind who can be silenced when the plot requires her silence. I have tried to show, however, that her speeches are full of sophisticated exploitations of conversational strategies which ought to make us reconsider her character and aban-don the construct of a Celia seen as an immature, childish, insecure young girl. Celia's function at Court is to provide a voice for the expression of disinterested friendship and true love, with the help of a set of sociolinguistic strategies known as positive politeness. In Arden, her function is different. She is there to foreground the ridiculous vein of much of Rosalind's behaviour. In their duologues, her wit and conversational expertise often contrast with Rosalind's stereotyped behaviour as arcadian lover. After all, not all of us like Rosalind best.

# And Then He Kissed Her:
## The Reclamation of Female Characters to Submissive Roles in Contemporary Fiction

### SHAN WAREING

### INTRODUCTION

Women's romance fiction has been the focus of considerable academic interest.[1] This study is concerned with contemporary fiction which has female central characters, and which appears to depart from many of the conventional features of romantic fiction. My hypothesis is that although the female protagonists of contemporary fiction may have very different public roles from the heroine of romance fiction of the past and present, it appears that romantic norms frequently still govern the way certain parts of novels are written – particularly romantic and sexual encounters.

This paper is a stylistic exploration of heterosexual romantic encounters and sex scenes in some works of modern fiction. It investigates the extent to which female characters, presented as assertive and independent in their daily lives are reclaimed in romantic encounters to the roles of passive romantic heroines.

## The Romance

While within the genre of the romance there are many variations and sub-categorisations to be made, it is nevertheless possible to supply the basic formula. The central character is a young, virginal woman. The focus of her attention is an older, richer, sexually experienced man of higher social standing than herself. This formula is to be found beneath the surface of such widely differing texts as Richardson's *Pamela*, Austen's *Pride and Prejudice*, Bronte's *Jane Eyre*, and du

---

[1] P.H. Mann, *A New Survey: the facts about romantic fiction* (Mills & Boon, London, 1974). John G. Cawelti, *Adventure, Mystery and Romance* (University of Chicago Press, Chicago, 1976). Janice Radway, *Reading the Romance* (University of North Carolina Press, London, 1984).

Maurier's *Rebecca*, as well as texts published by romance publishers such as Mills and Boon and Silhouette.

There are common psychological features to all these texts. The female character finds the male character's behaviour mysterious and domineering; his actions appear contradictory, his motives unfathomable. She constantly attempts to interpret his behaviour which alternates between tenderness and rejection. It is he who controls the erotic aspect of their relationship: he reveals to the female character her own desires. Her options are either to submit to him, or to bring about their separation. If she chooses separation, this ends when he seeks her out, confesses his real feelings, explains his previous behaviour and offers her love, marriage, and fidelity.

Terry Eagleton describes this plot structure as one which 'consolidates patriarchal power'.[2] Janice Radway responds similarly: 'Each romance is, in fact, a mythic account of how women must . . . achieve fulfillment in a patriarchal society.'[1] Both Eagleton and Radway see a strong causal link between patriarchal society, and the plot of the romance.

I propose that even fiction which does not obviously reproduce the romance plot can surreptitiously impose the norms of the romance on the love and sex lives of female protagonists, and that this is true of fiction of many genres. Most strikingly this occurs in love scenes, and it appears that certain stylistic features are typical of fictional portrayals of romance and sex. On examination of these stylistic features, when a plot synopsis would suggest an active, assertive, independent, intelligent female protagonist, romantic encounters are frequently written in such a way as to reinforce the patriarchal values found in the romance genre.

Certain aspects of texts are of particular interest in this respect and below I look at three aspects in turn. These are transitivity, focalization, and the fragmentation of characters into anatomical elements. I will combine theoretical discussion with textual analyses of relevant texts.

---

[2]  Terry Eagleton, *The Rape of Clarissa* (Blackwell, Oxford, 1984), p. 37.
[3]  Radway, op. cit., p. 17.

## TRANSITIVITY

. . . the different patterns of transitivity are the prime means of expressing our internal and external experiences, which is part of the ideational function of language.[4]

The concept of transitivity is primarily associated with Halliday's work in systemic linguistics from the late 1960s onwards.[5] The study of transitivity is concerned with how actions are represented: what kind of actions appear in a text, who does them, and to whom (or what). Succinctly this may be expressed as 'who (or what) does what to whom (or what)'. Through this dimension of language, stylisticians examine the extent to which a character is represented as having control over their environment. When writers make choices between different types of process and different participants, between the different roles participants might take, these decisions are realised through transitivity choices.

This system of analysing linguistic options in texts has been primarily concerned with the roles of human participants. A broad distinction is made to differentiate conscious actors, who are perceived as integral beings, capable of thought, communication, plans, and action, from everything else in the world, organic and inorganic, animate and inanimate, which is presumed not to be capable of conscious thought and planned action.

Verbs in English can be divided into categories, depending on the kind of activity they refer to, and the participants involved can be identified by terms which indicate the process and whether they are doing it, or having it done to them.

The first category I shall consider is that of 'material processes'. These are verbs which refer to some kind of obvious physical action, e.g. *We built our house, the moon shone, the child fell over*. The person/object that does the action is called 'the agent' (e.g. *We, the moon, the child*); the person/object the process is done to is called 'the affected entity' (e.g. *the house*).

The category is subdivided to make its application more precise or 'delicate'. The first division is between action processes and event

---

[4]  Katie Wales, A *Dictionary of Stylistics* (Longman, London, 1989), p. 446.
[5]  M.A.K. Halliday, 'Notes on transitivity and theme in English, part 1' in *Journal of Linguistics* 3, 1967, pp. 37–81, and later work.

processes. Event processes are usually concerned with non-human/in-
animate objects, e.g. *The moon shone, the jumper shrank.* Action processes are those in which human activities are involved, e.g. *we built
our house, the child fell over.* Action processes can be further divided
into intention processes and supervention processes, which helps to
distinguish between actions carried out deliberately by a human agent
(intention processes), e.g. *we built our house,* and actions which happen to people which they did not intend (supervention processes),
e.g. *the child fell over.* In the analyses which follow, when an anatomical element of a character (a hand, for example) is the agent in a
process, the process will be analysed as an event process, not an action
process, in keeping with the above definition.

The class of material processes can be shown in a schematic form as
follows:

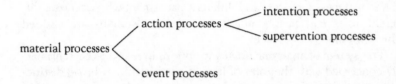

'Mental processes', the second category, are related in some way to
thought, opinions, ideas, or communication, e.g. *you saw me, they like
Austen, I said it, we have considered the issue.* Mental processes can be
similarly subdivided into internalised processes, such as *you saw me,
they like Austen, we have considered the issue;* and externalised processes, which usually involve some communication: *I said it, we wrote
the results up.* This can be represented diagrammatically as:

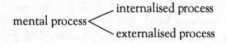

The actor in an internalised mental process is referred to as the
'senser', and what is thought about, or known by the senser, is called
the 'phenomenon'. In an externalised process, the actor is usually
called the 'sayer', and the person who is addressed is normally the
'recipient'.

The third category is that of 'relational processes' – these are
usually signalled by the verbs 'to be' or a verb indicating possession,
such as 'to have', e.g. *the wind is fresh, I have a pen.* These are 'states of

being', and the least 'active' kind of process. In the case of *the wind is fresh*, *the wind* is referred to as 'the carrier'; *fresh* is referred to as 'the attribute'. In the case of possession, as in *I have a pen*, the subject I is referred to as the 'possessor', and a *pen* is referred to as the 'possessed'.

The significance of these divisions is that choices made on a syntactic level are part of the representation of character. The extent to which a character is the passive 'victim' of circumstance, or is actively in control of their environment through making decisions and taking action, is one of the concerns of a feminist approach to stylistics.

If a character is very active in a text, in control of their own decisions and actions, an analysis of the text might be expected to show a range of processes, of which a relatively high number would be material action intention processes, where the character is performing actions which they have voluntarily chosen as a course of behaviour. On the other hand, a character whose behaviour consists of many internalised mental processes might appear oddly introspective. A combination of transitivity choices which consisted disproportionately of externalised mental processes would create a character who, for example, is always talking but never acting. If a character's behaviour is written as a sequence of supervention processes, the character is likely to appear not in control of what is happening to them.

Burton, in her analysis[6] of Sylvia Plath's novel *The Bell Jar*,[7] claims that Plath uses supervention processes to represent the narrator's behaviour with an unusually high frequency. Burton comments that: '[Plath's] texts abound in disenabling metaphors, disenabling lexis, and . . . disenabling syntactic structures'.[8] In support of her claim, Burton analyses an extract from *The Bell Jar* in which the narrator is in a hospital being prepared for electric shock treatment. An analysis of the clause structure supports the reading that the narrator is positioned as a passive 'victim', and the hospital staff have control over their environment and the narrator's, while the narrator has no control over what is happening to her.

This is one way to explore transitivity. The stylistician can demonstrate how a character who on first reading seems passive, a victim, not actively engaged in controlling their environment, is presented thus by the linguistic choices in the text. The character can then be

---

[6] Deirdre Burton, 'Through glass darkly: through dark glasses' in R. Carter, ed. *Language and Literature* (Allen & Unwin, London, 1982).

[7] Sylvia Plath, *The Bell Jar* (Faber & Faber, London, 1963).

[8] Burton, op. cit., p. 201.

compared with other characters in the text who appear to have more control over their environment, anticipating that this difference will be realised in a higher proportion of material action intention processes. To this end, Burton compares Plath's narrator to the nurse in the same extract, and her findings are indeed as predicted, that the nurse has many material action intention processes, in contrast to the narrator.

Another use of this method of analysis is to question the construction of a female character who is apparently assertive and in control of her life. The analysis can be used to monitor firstly whether the content of the text is supported or undermined by its syntactic choices, and secondly whether the character's behaviour reflects the characteristics which are generally typical of her in every aspect of her life as represented in the text.

## Examples of Transitivity

Romance scenes are an aspect of texts which is very fertile for transitivity analyses. In a heterosexual romance scene, where the transitivity choices support the gender relations of the 'romance' genre, as presented in the introduction, it is to be expected that the male protagonist will be the agent in material action intention processes more frequently than the female protagonist. She is more likely to be the actor in mental processes, or material event processes – making her appear physically passive and perhaps out of control of her actions. To illustrate how a text may be broken down into its transitivity choices, and to give some impression of what typical choices might be in a description of a heterosexual romance encounter, consider the following extract from Barbara Taylor Bradford's A Woman of Substance. This best-selling novel recounts the history of a kitchen maid, Emma Harte, who on the strength of her intelligence, determination, and hard work, becomes the owner of an international business corporation, and a multimillionaire. She has four children by four different men, but no enduring romantic relationship. In achieving financial success but not monogamous domesticity, she differs radically from the stereotypical heroine of the popular romance genre. However, this difference does not extend to the way she is written about in the bedroom. Below is an extract from the text, a scene between Emma and a new lover:

"Take your robe off, my love," he said softly as he came towards her. He covered her body with his own and cradled her in his arms, smiling down into her expectant face. "It's a pity to ruin this exotic hairdo", he murmured as he began to pull the pins from her hair. The russet tresses spilled around her shoulders, porcelain fragile and pink in the warm glow of the lamp, and he gasped at her loveliness now so perfectly revealed to him. He ran his hand through the heavy lengths and held her by the nape of the neck, bringing her face up to his own. His lips met hers, savouring their warmth and sweetness, and they were both engulfed by their longing and the emotions which had been denied release for weeks. He moved his mouth into the hollow of her neck, kissing her shoulders, her breasts and the deep valley between, and his strong hands smoothed over her firm skin and he caressed every part of her until he knew her fervour matched his own. Emma was suffused by an unfamiliar warmth, a burning heat that flooded her whole being. Her whole body arched up, cleaved to him. She ached to be joined to him, to become one with him, and she marvelled at her pleasure in his body and in her own . . .[9]

In order to analyse the transitivity choices in this passage, each clause is examined. The main verb in the clause is analysed as a process, and the actor is included in the analysis, as shown below. Notice that the content of the characters' speech has been disregarded.

| | |
|---|---|
| (a) he said | (k) his lips met hers |
| (b) he came towards her | (l) they were engulfed |
| (c) he covered her body | (m) he moved his mouth |
| (d) he cradled her | (n) his hands smoothed her skin |
| (e) he murmured | (o) he caressed her |
| (f) he began to pull | (p) he knew |
| (g) [her hair] spilled | (q) Emma was suffused |
| (h) he gasped | (r) her body arched |
| (i) he ran his hand through (her hair) | (s) she ached |
| (j) he held her | (t) she marvelled |

If we now add up the number of processes in which the male is the actor, and compare this with number in which the female is the actor, the results show a marked difference.

[9] Barbara Taylor Bradford, A Woman of Substance (Grafton, London, 1981), pp. 666–667.

Male (or male body part) as actor:

| | |
|---|---|
| (a) he said | = mental externalised |
| (b) he came towards her | = material action intention |
| (c) he covered her body | = material action intention |
| (d) he cradled her | = material action intention |
| (e) he murmured | = mental externalised |
| (f) he began to pull | = material action intention |
| (h) he gasped | = mental externalised |
| (i) he ran his hand through (her hair) | = material action intention |
| (j) he held her | = material action intention |
| (k) his lips met hers | = material action supervention |
| (body part as actor) | |
| (m) he moved his mouth | = material action intention |
| (n) his hands smoothed her skin | = material event |
| (body part as actor) | |
| (o) he caressed her | = material action intention |
| (p) he knew | = mental internalised |

Out of the twenty processes in the text, the male (or a male body part) is the actor in fourteen. If these are compared to the processes in which the female is the actor, the difference is striking.

Female (or female body part) as actor:

| | |
|---|---|
| (g) [her hair] spilled | = material event |
| (body part as actor) | |
| (q) Emma was suffused | = relational |
| (r) her body arched | = material event |
| (body part as actor) | |
| (s) she ached | = mental internalised |
| (t) she marvelled | = mental internalised |

There are five processes in which the female character, or parts of her body appear in the role of actor, in comparison with the fourteen processes in which the male, or parts of his body, appear are the actor. Furthermore, the processes performed by the female are different in kind from those performed by the male. In contrast to the eight material action intention processes in which the male is the agent, the female is agent in none. In the two material event processes in which she is the agent, parts of her body move independently of her volition (her hair spills and her body arches – these are responses, not actions she has chosen). The three remaining processes in which she is the actor are more passive in quality – to do with what she feels and what she thinks.

There is a strong correlation between the transitivity choices in the above text, and the representation of the female protagonist as the passive recipient of the male character's actions – she is not sexually active in her own right. While the male character's experience is represented in terms of the actions he does to her body, the female's experience is written about in terms of her thoughts and feelings, and her body's uncontrollable responses to the male character's sexual expertise.

In order to demonstrate further the workings of transitivity, consider this extract from Helen McInnes's spy novel, *Hidden Target*:

"I know more about myself than I ever did. I know that I – ". She raised her head, let her eyes meet his. I know that I love you, she ended silently. "Oh, Bob – " she held out her hand. He grasped it, took both her hands, held them tightly, felt her draw him near. His arms went around her, and he kissed her mouth, her eyes, her cheeks, her slender neck, her mouth again – long kisses lingering on slender lips. Her arms encircled him pressing him closer.[10]

If the processes and actors are abstracted from the text, the result is:

(a) she raised her head
(b) (she) let her eyes
(c) she ended silently
(d) she held out her hand
(e) he grasped it
(f) (he) took both her hands
(g) (he) held them tightly
(h) (he) felt her draw him near
(i) his arms went round her
(j) he kissed her mouth
(k) her arms encircled him

Five of these processes have the female character, or parts of her body, as the actor; six have the male, or his body parts, as the actor.

Having identified the actors and processes, we can label them. The processes with the female as actor are:

(a) she raised her head          = material action intention
                                   (affected = female body part)
(b) she let her eyes meet his    = material action intention
                                   (affected = female body part)
(c) she ended silently           = mental internalised
(d) she held out her hand        = material action intention
                                   (affected = female body part)
(e) her arms encircled him       = material event (affected = male)
    (actor = female body part)

---

10 Helen McInnes, *Hidden Target* (Collins, Glasgow, 1982), p. 315.

Those processes which have the male in the role of actor are:

| | |
|---|---|
| (e) he grasped it | = material action intention (affected = female body part) |
| (f) (he) took both her hands | = material action intention (affected = female body part) |
| (g) (he) held them tightly | = material action intention (affected = female body part) |
| (h) (he) felt her draw him near | = mental internalised |
| (i) his arms went around her (actor = male body part) | = material event (affected = female) |
| (j) he kissed her mouth | = material action intention (affected = female body part) |

Now that we have a scheme of the transitivity choices in the text, we can compare the representations of the female and male characters, in terms of 'who does what to whom'. The female is the actor in five processes, compared to the six in which the male is the actor. She is the agent in three material action intention processes, compared to the four in which the male is the agent, and body parts of both the female and the male are agents in one material event process. They are also both sensers in one internalised mental process. While these results show little difference between the two characters, there is a striking imbalance observable in the affected entities of the material processes. In the five processes where the male (or male body part) is the agent, four processes are done to parts of the female's body (*her hand/s*, *her mouth*), and the fifth to her as a whole (*His arms went around her*). Yet when the female character (or her body parts) is the agent, the affected entity is the male on only one occasion (*her arms encircled him*). In the three material action intention processes in which the female protagonist is the agent, the affected entity is a part of her own body: *her head, her eyes, her hand*.

So in this text there is not a great discrepancy between the kinds, or quantities, of processes in which the female and male characters are actors. There is, however, a marked difference between the way the affected entity slot is filled. The female, or her body parts, is on the receiving end of eight of nine material processes, whether she or the male character is the agent. The male is the affected entity only once, and in a material event process, where the female's arms appear to act 'independently'.

In this section I have shown how gender roles can be embedded in texts even at the level of their syntactic relations, and that an analysis of the transitivity choices can be used to identify this phenomenon.

## FOCALIZATION

The second aspect of romance scenes I will consider is focalization. The concept of focalization provides a means of identifying the consciousness through which a fictional event is presented in an text.

The focalizer is most likely to be a fictional character within the world of the text, or an external narrator. The important difference between focalization and 'point of view' is that, while the point of view can be that of an external narrator, a scene may still give precedence to the perception of one character, rather than another's. Thus a scene may be focalized by one character rather than another, even if the point of view is that of an external narrator. Mieke Bal, who coined the term, describes its textual effect, and the value of an analytic practise which can handle it, as follows:

> As any 'vision' presented can have a strongly manipulative effect, and is, consequently, very difficult to extract from the emotions, not only from those attributed to the focalizer and the character, but also from those of the reader, a technical term will help us to keep our attention on the technical side of such a means of manipulation.[11]

With regard to the degrees of focalization, Rimmon-Kenan[12] proposes three distinctions: fixed, variable, and multiple focalization. This allows an analysis to differentiate focalization which remains fixed throughout the narrative, which alternates between two predominant focalizers, and which shifts among several focalizers. The important point to extract from this is that focalization need not remain with a single character, or narrator-focalizer, but can shift in the course of a text.

[11] Mieke Bal, *Narratology: introduction to the theory of narrative* (University of Toronto Press, London, 1986), p. 102.
[12] Shlomith Rimmon-Kenan, *Narrative Fiction: contemporary poetics* (Routledge, London, 1983), p. 75.

*Examples of Focalization*

The first two examples are to demonstrate two possible relations between the narrative voice and the centre of focalization. In the first text below, the narrator and the focalizer coincide. In Donna Tartt's novel *The Secret History*, the male narrator, Richard, is a character in the story, and the narrative is told in the first person. The emotions, the perspective from which the world is seen, belong to the narrator-focalizer, and it is his view of events which the reader has immediate access to.

> We walked a good distance around the lake's edge, she and I, then started back. Camilla, one hand shading her light-dazzled eyes, was telling me a long story about something the dog had done [. . .] but I wasn't following her very closely: she looked so much like her brother, yet his straightforward, uncompromising good looks were almost magical when repeated, with only slight variations, in her. She was a living reverie for me: the mere sight of her sparked an almost infinite range of fantasy, from Greek to Gothic, from vulgar to divine.[13]

This is clearly Richard's view of Camilla, not Camilla's view of herself – her experience of the conversation is not imparted to us, as it is not known to Richard.

This situation, where the reader is provided with one character's view of events and not another's, not only occurs in first person narrator-focalizer narratives, however. Colin Dexter's detective novel *The Way Through the Woods* is narrated in the third person; the narrative voice is external to the story, not one of the characters involved in it. The focalization in the following extract also lies with the male protagonist, David Michaels.

> She said nothing more; and he wondered for a while whether it would be sensible to go down and make a couple of cups of piping-hot coffee for them, and then perhaps turn on the bedside lamp and look upon his lovely bride. But there was no need. Seemingly Cathy Michaels had accepted the logic of his words, and her mind was more at ease; and soon he felt the silky caress of her inner thigh against him.[14]

[13] Donna Tartt, *The Secret History* (Penguin, London, 1992), p. 112.
[14] Colin Dexter, *The Way Through the Woods* (Pan, London, 1992, this ed. 1993), p. 126.

As readers we have access to David's thought processes and feelings (*he wondered, he felt*), but not to Cathy's (*seemingly [she] had accepted . . . and her mind was more at ease*); what is going on in her mind is as opaque to us as it is to David. We, like him, have only her external signals to go on. As readers, therefore, it is David's view of events which we share, although the narrator is external.

Scenes in fiction are often focalized through one of the characters present, and that character's vision of events is therefore privileged over that of other characters. The significance of this phenomenon for the current analysis is that in romance and sexual encounters, it is frequently the male who focalizes the scene, and the female's experience is omitted.

Consider the following sentences from A *Woman of Substance*.

Paul finally took her to him with flaring passion, his ardour gentled but in no way muted by his tenderness. Silken arms and legs entwined him, fluid and weightless, yet they pulled him down . . . down . . . down.[15]

The narrative voice is external and omniscient. It is not present in the text as a fictional character but is external; yet it can reveal the characters' motivations and thoughts to the readers. Theoretically, therefore, the narrative is reported by a disembodied voice which can record objectively the course of events and the psychology of the characters. However, the 'vision' is Paul's: it is his experience of the event which is narrated. Emma is present not as her own consciousness, but as Paul experiences her – as disembodied limbs, 'silken arms and legs', without weight or form, 'fluid and weightless'. A further linguistic signal that it is Paul's consciousness from which the event is focalized is that the pronouns 'he' and 'she' suggest a subject which has unity of mind and body. In the case of Emma, however, the pronoun 'they' is used, referring to her limbs. Her body has been separated from her consciousness. Her body is present in the narrative as focalized by Paul: her unified consciousness is not available to the reader. This aspect of texts – 'fragmentation' – will be looked at in more detail in the next section.

By focalizing the scene through the male's experience, the female is inevitably represented as the object of the male gaze. By mediating

15 Taylor Bradford, op. cit., p. 667.

her textual representation through the male's perception of her, her sexual pleasure is represented as subordinate to his.

Heterosexual sex in fiction of course does not have to be focalized from the perspective of the male. Exactly the opposite occurs in the following lines from Toni Morrison's novel *Sula*:

> There in the pantry, empty now of flour sacks, void of row upon row of canned goods, free for ever of strings of tiny green peppers, holding the wet milk bottle tight in her arm she stood wide-legged against the wall and pulled from his track-lean hips all the pleasure her thighs could hold.[16]

Focalized from Sula's centre of consciousness, not only is the female protagonist represented as unified (*she stood*), while the male is re-duced to anatomical elements (*his track-lean hips*), but the whole environment is evidence of the domestic life which co-exists with Sula's sexual life.

The plot of the novel *Sula* challenges stereotypical representations of race, gender, and sexuality, and therefore it is perhaps not unex-pected to find that this scene has significant stylistic differences from the encounters discussed above.

However, it is only when Sula's sexual power is in the ascendancy that she is the focalizer in her sexual encounters. She later loses the emotional independence and sexual control she exerts in the early stages of the affair (as typified in the encounter reproduced above). As she inclines towards the security of domesticity, dependency, and monogamy, the centre of focalization shifts from Sula to Ajax, the male protagonist.

> He stood up and mounted the stairs with her, and entered the spotless bathroom where the dust had been swept from underneath the claw-foot tub. He was trying to remember the date of the air show in Drayton. As he came into the bedroom, he saw Sula lying on fresh white sheets, wrapped in the deadly odour of freshly ap-plied cologne.
>
> He dragged her underneath him and made love to her with the steadiness and intensity of a man about to leave for Drayton.[17]

Focalization has switched to the male protagonist. It is his, rather

16 Toni Morrison, *Sula* (Grafton, London, 1982), p. 113.
17 Morrison, op. cit., p. 120.

than Sula's, mental activities which are revealed to the reader, and his emotions that colour the scene. Ajax tries to remember the date of the air show; he is planning to leave. Sula's thoughts and actions are excluded from the scene, being unknown to Ajax, and therefore unknown to the reader. A second indication that focalization resides with Ajax is that Ajax 'sees' Sula lying on the sheets: she is perceived by him, so it is literally his vision that has precedence. Furthermore, Ajax is the agent in the material action intention processes *He stood up and mounted the stairs*; Sula accompanies him, an accessory to his actions, not an actor in her own right. However, perhaps the strongest indication that the scene is focalized by Ajax is the use of the adjective 'deadly'. Only so far as Ajax is concerned is the cologne 'deadly', because for him it indicates the threat posed by Sula to his freedom. Sula wears the cologne to attract, not repel, him; the adjective cannot emerge from her perspective of the scene.

In summary, there are signals in the text indicating whether a character is functioning as the centre of focalization, and this does not necessarily coincide with the narrative voice, although it may. The focalizer is not necessarily static, but can shift from one internal character to another, or to an external narrator. The importance of the concept of focalization is that it slants the emotive and ideological content of a text, and represents the experience of the protagonists partially.

Thus focalization is a very effective way of giving precedence to the perspective of one character rather than another. It is frequently used to present the female protagonist as a passive object for male consumption, as in the extract from *A Woman of Substance*. In the extracts from *Sula*, it is used to show which character is dominant in the relationship, switching from Sula to Ajax as the power swings from the one to the other.

One of the textual signals which I have suggested indicates where focalization lies, is that the focalizer is represented as a unified subject, while other characters may be fragmented into body parts, their physical selves disconnected from their thoughts and emotions. It is this aspect of texts which I will consider in greater depth in the next section.

## FRAGMENTATION

The technique of fragmenting the female body in pornographic literature has been widely noted (see especially Kappeler).[18] This has two effects. Firstly the body is depersonalised, objectified, reduced to its parts. Secondly, a consequence of fragmentation is that in most circumstances a fragmented character cannot be the scene's focalizer, so their personal experience is written out of the scene.

Fragmentation of the female protagonist in sex and romance scenes is therefore connected to male focalization; the female is represented as an object, or collection of objects, for the male gaze.

The convention of referring to a protagonist as anatomic elements is not without its defendants. For example, Derek Attridge argues that what he terms 'organic liberation' in a text results in 'erotic arousal':

> Sexuality thrives on the separation of the body into independent parts, whereas a sexually repressive morality insists on the wholeness and singleness of body and mind or soul.[19]

This argument, however, totally ignores the gender inequalities which occur in such representations. Female characters are represented as anatomical elements far more frequently than male characters are. This is true not only of pornographic material, but of advertising images, romance fiction, love poetry, and love scenes generally in mainstream fiction. The following sonnet by Thomas Nabbes is typical of the way the female is 'dismembered' by the text, her physical attributes described as if they were separate entities:

> Her real worth
> What though with figures I should raise
> Above all height my Mistress' praise,
> Calling her cheek a blushing rose.
> The fairest June did e'er disclose,
> Her forehead lilies, and her eyes
> The luminaries of the skies;
> That on her lips ambrosia grows,

---

[18] Susanne Kappeler, *The Pornography of Representation* (Polity Press, Cambridge, 1986).

[19] Derek Attridge, *Peculiar Language: literature as difference from the Renaissance to James Joyce* (Methuen, London, 1988), p. 167.

And from her kisses nectar flows?
Too great hyperboles! unless
She loves me, she is none of these,
But if her heart and her desires
Do answer mine with equal fires
These attributes are then too poor;
She is all these and ten times more.[20]

Writing of this kind, where the female is identified by anatomic elements such as cheeks, forehead, eyes, and lips, is very common in poetry, and also in fiction, as will be seen in the examples from novels below.

## Examples of Fragmentation

The passage quoted previously from Helen McInnes' *Hidden Target.* reveals the same kind of fragmentation to be seen in the poem above, and which is associated by Kappeler with pornography, and by Attridge with 'erotic arousal':

> She raised her head, let her eyes meet his. . . . She held out her hand. He grasped it, took both her hands, held them tightly, felt her draw him near. His arms went around her, and he kissed her mouth, her eyes, her cheeks, her slender neck, her mouth again – long kisses lingering on yielding lips. Her arms encircled him, pressing him closer . . .[21]

In this extract, anatomical elements of the male are referred to only twice, in the expressions *her eyes met his* (nominal ellipsis of 'eyes'), and *his arms*. References are made to anatomical elements of the female twelve times, however: *her head, her eyes, her hand, her hands, them* (her hands), *her mouth, her eyes, her neck, her mouth, lips,* and *her arms*. The marked difference in this distribution reflects the conventions of representation of female and male protagonists.

Focalization in the poem 'Her real worth' clearly resides with the male poet-narrator. In the McInnes extract above, it also resides with the male character. The narrator in the McInnes extract is external to

[20] Thomas Nabbes (1612–1645), 'Her real worth' in A *Treasury of Seventeenth Century Verse*, ed. H.J. Massingham (Macmillan, London, 1941).
[21] McInnes, op. cit., pp. 314–315.

the text and therefore could theoretically give an impartial account of the scene, not prioritising the experience of either protagonist, and not fragmenting one character more than the other. However, the text does not do this, but follows the conventions for writing about fictional heterosexual encounters. Not only is the female protagonist fragmented while the male protagonist is not, but the adjectives applied to the female protagonist (*slender* and *yielding*) also indicate she is an object being viewed by the male protagonist.

Having observed that fragmentation of the female protagonist tends to co-occur with male focalization, it is worth illustrating what a text might look like which exploits different forms of representation. The following extract is from *The Vagabond* by Colette. The eroticism of this text does explore the 'organic liberation' to which Attridge refers, but differs substantially from the passage by McInnes because focalization resides with the female protagonist rather than the male, and the fragmentation of the body into anatomic elements occurs roughly equally for both protagonists.

> I move my head imperceptibly, because of his moustache which brushes against my nostrils with a scent of vanilla and honeyed tobacco. Oh! . . . suddenly my mouth, in spite of itself, lets itself be opened, opens of itself as irresistibly as a ripe plum splits in the sun. And once again there is born that exacting pain which spreads from my lips, all down my flanks as far as my knees, that swelling as of a wound which wants to open once more and overflow – the voluptuous pleasure that I had forgotten.
>
> I let the man who has awakened me drink the fruit he is pressing. My hands, stiff a moment ago, lie soft and warm in his, and my body, as I lie back, strives to mould itself to his. Drawn close by the arm which holds me, I burrow deeper into his shoulder and press myself against him, taking care not to separate our lips . . .[22]

The eight references to anatomic elements of the female (*my head, my nostrils, my mouth, my lips, my flanks, my knees, my hands, my body*) are accompanied by five equivalent references to the male (*his moustache, his* (hands), *his* (body), *the arm, his shoulder*), and focalization resides totally with the female character-narrator.

Colette does exploit the eroticism of fragmentation in this extract; the text however breaks with the pattern which dominated the texts

---

[22] Colette, *The Vagabond* (1911, this ed. translated from the original French, Secker & Warburg, London, 1954), pp. 126–127.

previously analysed. Fragmentation occurs, but there is not the marked imbalance which was noticeable in previous texts: both protagonists are fragmented. Neither in this instance is fragmentation associated with male focalization. The female character is the focalizer, and it is her pleasure which dominated the text – it is the male's sensations and thoughts which are not represented. Furthermore, an analysis of the transitivity choices reveals a distribution quite dissimilar from those discussed in the extracts from *A Woman of Substance* and *Hidden Target*.

Female (or female body part) as actor

| | |
|---|---|
| I move my head | = material action intention (affected = female body part) |
| my mouth . . . lets itself be opened | = material event (affected = female body part) |
| [I had forgotten] the voluptuous pleasure | = mental internalised |
| I let the man | = material action intention (affected = male) |
| My hands lie | = material event |
| my body strives to mould itself | = material event |
| I lie back | = material action intention |
| I burrow deeper | = material action intention |
| [I] press myself | = material action intention (affected = female) |

Male (or male body part) as actor

| | |
|---|---|
| his moustache . . . brushes | = material event |
| [the man] has awakened me | = material action intention |

Processes without human actors

| | |
|---|---|
| a ripe plum splits | = material event |
| [that exacting pain] is born | = material event |
| [that exacting pain] spreads from my lips | = material event |
| a wound . . . wants to open and overflow | = mental internalised |

The female protagonist is the actor in nine processes, the male protagonist is the actor in two. There are four processes that do not have a human character, or body part, in the role of actor. Five of the nine processes in which the female protagonist is the actor are material action intention processes. There are three material event processes, and one internalised mental process. The male protagonist is the actor in one material action intention process, and one material event process. Overall there are seven material event processes, out of a total of 15 when the metaphors with non-human actors are included – almost half. In preceding analyses, I have argued that material event processes are used to represent a world in which the actors are not fully in control of their actions. In this scene too, there is a sense of both inaction, and inevitability – neither protagonist appears to be controlling the situation.

This is an alternative way to organise the transitivity choices, focalization and fragmentation of a love scene. Neither character is represented as dominant, controlling the passive partner's sexual responses. Focalization resides with the female protagonist, so her pleasure is foregrounded in the text, not omitted as happens so frequently. Fragmentation is applied equally to both protagonists, and so the inequality typical of many texts, and of pornographic ones in particular, is no longer an issue.

This is clearly not the only alternative way to organise these stylistic choices: many other possibilities obviously exist. What I have tried to show is how infrequently such alternatives are explored in contemporary fiction writing, and how deeply embedded the stylistic conventions are relating to sexual and romantic encounters.


## CONCLUSION

My aim has been to provide a stylistic framework for exploring how female characters are recuperated into a traditional passive role in sexual and romantic encounters, even when the characters appear to subvert or reject patriarchal values in other areas of their lives. From the analyses above, it is evident that the tradition of the passive heroine is deeply rooted in the norms of novel writing. The stylistic patterns which are most frequently used in the representation of a female protagonist create her as the object, and not the originator, of desire, and view her through the eyes of a male observer, fragmenting her body for his speculation.

However, it is also clear that these are not the only choices available to authors who write heterosexual love scenes. The extracts discussed above by Toni Morrison and Colette are evidence that romantic and sexual encounters in fiction can be reshaped. These extracts indicate that different combinations of linguistic forms can be used, and that in different contexts, the old forms can have new meanings. The stylistic patterns which represent female subordination can be altered.

# Close Encounters of a Feminist Kind: Transitivity Analysis and Pop Lyrics

## SARA MILLS

### Introduction

The aim of this chapter is to evaluate critically a form of close feminist textual analysis – the analysis of transitivity choices, that is, who
does what to whom in a text. Following from Deirdre Burton's influential essay on transitivity, I will set this type of analysis within a
wider framework of feminist textual analysis and consider some of the
advantages of a close textual analysis in general for feminist work.[1] I
will also consider some of the difficulties which this type of work
engenders, and propose a model of feminist analysis which is prepared
to acknowledge some of the difficulties of attributing straightforward
meanings to sets of language items.[2] In order to explore these general
questions about feminist analysis, I will firstly consider transitivity
analysis as it has been undertaken within critical stylistics and then go
on to consider feminist transitivity analysis; then I will focus my
analysis on the lyrics of a pop song, Hit by the Sugar Cubes, to
demonstrate that transitivity analysis can yield complex insights into
reading a text. Rather than simply assuming that we can interpret
transitivity choices as having particular meanings, I argue in the
analysis and in the chapter as a whole that transitivity choices, like
other linguistic choices, have a range of meanings dependent on the
context in which they occur and the presuppositions which the reader
brings to bear on the interpretative process.

---

[1]  D. Burton, 'Through glass darkly: through dark glasses: on stylistics and
political commitment', in R. Carter, ed., Language and Literature (Allen and
Unwin, London, 1982), pp. 195–214.

[2]  This is a revised version of a section from Feminist Stylistics (Routledge,
London, 1994); the ideas in the article were first presented at the Nottingham University Systemics conference, 1993, where I received some very
useful and insightful feedback, particularly from Margaret Berry.

*Critical Stylistics*

Since the 1970s a form of stylistic analysis has developed which is openly political; this has developed in direct reaction to a great deal of writing within stylistics as a whole which attempts to masquerade as simply an objective and neutral form of analysis.[3] As Deirdre Burton states: 'any writer that supposes that he or she is politically neutral in their writing is merely naively supporting and demonstrating the (largely unseen and unnoticed) political bias of the status quo.'[4] With collections of essays such as Fowler et al.'s *Language and Control*,[5] there was a move to consider the possibility of analysing the language of a text without losing sight of a reason for doing the analysis. The aim was not to engage in simple number-crunching, that is the counting of types of clauses with no other motivation than to find out the number of clauses in a text; rather, the avowed aim of these critics was to find out something about the systematic lexical *choices* which they discovered in texts. Readers in general were not consciously aware of these systematic choices, but they were traces of larger ideological frameworks which influenced readers' thinking in general. Through analysis of these linguistic choices, the critical linguist could enable the reader to develop ways of reading which were truly critical, that is, which would 'see through' language to the underlying ideological positions of which they had not previously been aware. Their view of language could be best summed up by the following statement by David Lee: 'Given that language is an instrument for the assignment of phenomena of human experience to conceptual categories it is clearly not simply a mirror that reflects reality. Rather, its function is to impose structure on our perceptions of the world. Language is also

---

[3]  It is quite easy to identify the reasons for the development of a form of language analysis which characterised itself as objective: for example, the unstable position of linguistics as a science; the reaction towards a very subjective approach to literature current in the 1970s in English departments; and the growing tendency towards scientificity and theory within English departments. However, there were many critics who viewed this move towards seeming objectivity as a collusion with many elements in literary analysis which were non-progressive: for example, a concentration on canonical texts; a refusal to consider context; a refusal to acknowledge the role of the reader; and a stress on the authority of the individual critic.

[4]  Burton, op. cit. (1982), p. 197.

[5]  R. Fowler, G. Kress, R. Hodge, and T. Trew, *Language and Control* (Routledge and Kegan Paul, London, 1979).

highly selective, and in this sense, too, the process of linguistic encoding involves a significant degree of abstraction away from "reality".[6]

For many of the early stylisticians, language analysis was simply a way of 'firming up' intuitions about a text, and of ensuring replicability of results. For those critics who began to develop analyses under the heading 'critical linguistics', there was a sense in which those very intuitions were themselves suspect: you came out of the analysis of a text with exactly the suspicions that you had when you went in. Furthermore, critical linguists began to investigate the ways in which those intuitions themselves were formed and where they originated. Viewing texts within a larger political analysis of society, these critics determined to develop a range of analytical skills with which people could interrogate texts.[7] For all of these critics, there is an assumption that ideology and language are crucially linked, following on from theoretical work of the Marxist critic Louis Althusser.[8] Ideology is viewed as a set of representations of reality which occur in a variety of contexts and which inform people's thinking about who they are and what their role in society is. These representations are, for Althusser, necessarily distorted and represent the interests of the ruling classes. Althusser suggested that our everyday thoughts, which feel to us as if they are personal and originate out of our own volition and decision-making, are in fact informed by ideology. Ideological knowledges become our knowledges through the process whereby texts of all kinds call upon us – they address us as individuals to recognise that these ideological representations are 'true'. It is in the repeated calling upon individuals to recognise certain ideological representations as 'common-sense' or 'natural' that these knowledges become our own. Language is the site where these ideological representations are both enacted, processed and personalised, and it is also, for critical linguists, the place where individuals can learn to unpick and challenge this process.[9]

For later critical linguists, there was a necessity for differentiating

---

6 D. Lee, *Competing Discourses: Perspective and Ideology in Language* (Longman, London, 1992), p. 8.
7 Norman Fairclough's *Language and Power* (Longman, London, 1989) is a good example of this trend towards teaching skills of analysis in order to unpick the underlying ideologies of the text.
8 L. Althusser, *Essays on Ideology* (Verso, London, 1984).
9 For a fuller account of this process, see S. Mills, 'Knowing your place: a Marxist feminist stylistic analysis', in M. Toolan, ed., *Language Text and Context: Essays in Stylistics* (Routledge, London, 1992), pp. 182–208.

between synoptic and dynamic models of ideology. A synoptic view of ideology sees individual speakers as being forced into certain lexical choices and therefore into certain viewpoints or world-views. This sees the relation between language choice and the individual as one of coercion, and the role of the speaker as being at the mercy of larger social forces. With the dynamic model, by contrast, as Martin states, 'ideology can be interpreted more as a type of language dependent on the use to which language is put. Here we are looking at ideology in crisis, undergoing a process of change during which speakers take up options to challenge or defend some world-view that has prevailed to that point in time.'[10] It is this type of dynamic model of ideology which I will be drawing on later in this chapter in order to formulate the ways in which critical linguistics might be useful for feminist text analysis.

As well as signalling a move away from traditional concerns with the beauty of the language of literary texts to a concern with the ideology encoded therein, the essays in Fowler et al.'s *Language and Control* signalled a move towards an analysis which viewed literary texts within the context of other types of writing, for example, newspapers, advertisements, and birthday cards.[11] It was thought that the elitism often entailed in the analysis of literary texts would be replaced with a concern with the artifacts of everyday life. In this way, analysts would be able to investigate the workings of ideology at a much more critical and perhaps unnoticed level: whilst it was 'commonsense' to analyse literary texts, advertisements were at the time only beginning to be analysed by critics within cultural and media studies. Feminist analysts have been particularly notable in this area, since women are positioned very much as the consumers of popular culture par excellence.[12]

During the 1970s this form of critical linguistics attempted to demonstrate the ways in which this type of analysis could be tied into linguistic frameworks, particularly the grammatical theory of Michael Halliday. Halliday's linguistics proposed that language was embedded

10 J.R. Martin, 'Grammaticalising ecology: the politics of baby seals and kangaroos', in T. Threadgold, E. Grosz, G. Kress, M. Halliday, *Language, Semiotics, Ideology* (Sydney Studies in Society and Culture, No. 3, 1986), pp. 225–268, esp. p. 228.
11 See, for further work in this area, M. Montgomery, A. Durant, N. Fabb, T. Furniss, S. Mills, *Ways of Reading* (Routledge, London, 1992).
12 See J. Williamson, *Decoding Advertisements: Ideology and Meaning in Advertising* (Marion Boyars, London, 1983).

in and not separate from society. As Fowler states: 'The forms of language in use are a part of as well as a consequence of social process': that is, not only does society and societal norms construct language but language itself has an effect on what happens in society and its norms.[13] This is a particularly useful move away from the debates around linguistic determinism whereby certain language forms are seen to cause certain ways of thinking; this new more complex model of language could show that there was a very complex and close-knit relation between language and society.

Halliday himself wrote several essays of linguistic analysis of literature, and his views on linguistic analysis were also taken up by numerous stylisticians.[14] There was a tendency in this early work to be rather functionalist, that is, to decide on a mode of analysis and apply it to the text without a consideration of the possibility of a plurality of meanings to particular language items. This early work was criticised later by Kress and Hodge, where they argued for greater flexibility in the interpretation of results and a greater concentration on other factors which determine the meaning of items for readers.[15] In short, they argued that there was not a simple relation between form and function, although there were clearly parameters within which a preponderance of particular elements could be analysed to have a restricted range of meanings. This problem of the relation between patterns in language choice and linguistic function is most notable in the work of linguists on transitivity, and it is a problem which forms the focus of the analysis later in this chapter.

## Transitivity Analysis

One of the most interesting areas of discussion within critical linguistics has been that of transitivity analysis, the analysis of the roles and types of verbs/processes which characters within texts repeatedly use. Halliday himself conducted a linguistic analysis of transitivity choices in William Golding's novel, *The Inheritors*.[16] In this analysis, he tries

---

[13] Fowler et al., op. cit. (1979), p. 26.
[14] See M.A.K. Halliday, 'Linguistic function and literary style: an inquiry into the language of William Golding's *The Inheritors*', in S. Chatman, *Literary Style: A Symposium* (OUP, London, 1971), pp. 330–65; and also R. Carter, ed., *Language and Literature* (Allen and Unwin, London, 1982).
[15] G. Kress and B. Hodge, *Social Semiotics* (Polity/Blackwell, London, 1988).
[16] Halliday, op. cit. (1971).

to link the systematic choices which Golding makes for his characters with the creation of a world-view. Transitivity for Halliday is 'the set of options whereby the speaker encodes his [sic] experience of the process of the external world, and of the internal world of his consciousness, together with the participants in these processes and their attendant circumstances; and it embodies a very basic distinction of processes into two types, those that are regarded as due to an external cause, an agency other than the person or object involved and those that are not.'[17] Thus, Halliday is concerned with the representation of *who acts* (who is an agent) and who is *acted upon* (who is affected by the actions of others). This view of transitivity forming a coherent world-view can quite easily be translated into concerns about the ways that language and ideology are interrelated.

In discussions of transitivity, there are a range of choices which are available and these revolve around three sets of choices: material, mental and relational.[18] In this system, processes can be categorised into those elements which are actions which can be observed in the real world and which have consequences [material]: for example, 'she *swam* across the river'; those which take place largely in the mind [mental]: for example, 'she *thought* about the situation'; and those which simply relate two elements together [relational]: for example, 'it *is* rather cold'. Within material action processes, there are two further choices, between 'material action intention' and 'material action supervention'; with material action intention, there is a clear will to do something: for example, 'I broke the window, in order to get into the house', but with supervention there is an attempt to capture for analysis those verbal processes where things are not done intentionally, for example, 'I broke my favourite glasses'.

An analysis of transitivity consists of counting the ratios of choice of types of process; therefore, if an author or speaker consistently chooses mental processes, a particular type of text will be produced. The main emphasis in this type of analysis is that in producing text, there are a range of choices to be made, and every text which has

17 Ibid., p. 359.
18 There are a number of different forms of transitivity analysis whereby the range and number of categories differ: some making a separate 'textual' category, and some subsuming this within mental process. The main focus of this type of analysis rests essentially the same despite differences in terminology. [See Fowler, Martin and Lee, op. cit., for different frameworks.] I have used Burton's 1982 simplified framework here.

been produced could have been produced differently. In his 1971 essay, Halliday demonstrates that analysis of the systematic use of certain types of transitivity choice can help us as readers to distinguish between world-views; in this case, the world-views of characters in Golding's novel. Halliday shows how one group of characters in the novel uses a form of language whereby agency is attributed to inanimate objects rather than people. Halliday argues that these choices about agency embody a view of the world whereby these characters operate within but not on nature, where they are in some senses the recipients of actions rather than the instigators. Thus, by analysing patterns in transitivity choice it is possible to make more general statements about the way that characters view their position in the world and their relation to others.

## Transitivity Analysis and Feminist Critics

Deirdre Burton's work on transitivity has inspired a range of feminist work which tried to make use of linguistic accounts in order to see the way that world-views were created for women by writers.[19] Burton does a very simple transitivity analysis of a passage from Sylvia Plath's novel *The Bell Jar* to demonstrate that the female protagonist (who in the passage chosen is being given electric shock therapy), is written into a particularly disenabling role by the author. This is a role which is quite common for female characters within novels – that of passivity and thought, rather than one of action and acting upon other characters. The protagonist does not use material action intention processes; instead, it is the other characters in the text who act upon her. Burton's conclusions from this type of analysis are complex; she concludes that women are often represented in particular disenabling ways, even by women writers; this has become part of the common-sense knowledge of our culture which we do not necessarily question, namely, that women are represented as passive and acted upon. She shows that in rewriting the transitivity choices you entail a rewriting of the content as well. For her there is an extremely close link between form and function. Other feminist critics such as Shan Wareing have attempted to use this framework to analyse other texts to similar effect, analysing the way that women are represented in popular

---

[19] Burton, op. cit. (1982).

fiction.[20] These critics have shown that even when there are strong female characters in a text, who are represented with predominantly material action processes, when the characters are represented in a sexual or emotional sphere, there is a clear switch to women as acted-upon. This would lead us to assume that in the sexual or romantic sphere there is a strong ideological pressure which means that women can only be conceptualised as passive, or as not in control.

## Feminism and Ideology

For many feminists, women are particularly subjected to the effects of ideology. In many ways, it is clear that there are a range of belief systems about women which do not 'fit' with the reality of women's lives. These systems of belief are not simply imposed upon women, but women themselves actively take part in them and appropriate and reject them according to their investments and interests in them.[21] In this way, it is possible to see ideology as something which is not unitary, but which is negotiated by individual agents. An ideology, in this view, is a sequence or set of statements which have certain conceptual links, but which individual subjects will negotiate, affirm and/or resist. This point is quite important in relation to the analysis of language in texts, because it is essential that we do not see particular language items or statements necessarily having one undisputed meaning which is recognised by all readers.[22] Similarly, language items do not 'make sense' in isolation, but only when they are set in the context of larger scale ideological frameworks and frameworks of critique.[23]

[20] S. Wareing, 'Women in fiction: stylistic modes of reclamation', in *Parlance*, 2, 2 (1990), pp. 72–85; and her chapter in this volume.
[21] For a fuller discussion of this point, see W. Hollway, 'Gender difference and the production of subjectivity', in H. Crowley and S. Himmelweit, eds., *Knowing Women* (Polity/Open University, Cambridge, 1992), pp. 240–274.
[22] As I have argued elsewhere, Mills, op. cit. (1992), there may be a dominant interpretation to a text, but this is one which may be resisted.
[23] To make this point clear, we might like to consider the phrase 'unmarried mother'. This makes sense not in isolation, but only within a larger framework where there are other statements which have implicit assumptions about women's roles as mothers, father's roles as providers, the function of marriage as the correct, approved site for reproduction, and as women's ultimate goal [therefore women are either married or unmarried]; and where there are a range of other associated statements about welfare provision

The set of myths or ideologies around romantic love and emotions are just one area where ideology affects women's lives in a way in which the effect is not so great on men.[24] The ideology of romantic love, in Mills and Boon romances, for example, whereby romance is seen as the most important element in a woman's life and where women are literally taken over by passionate feelings, has been naturalised within our culture, so that it is sometimes difficult to 'see around' it. A great number of pop songs portray romantic love as a form of pain and suffering which women should take pleasure in.[25] Women are constructed in different ways to men within pop songs and in culture in general, and the notion of who is in control is central to this ideological gender difference, since generally women are represented as passive 'recipients' of love and men are represented as 'agents'.[26] In many pop songs, women are portrayed as out of

which view single women with children as burdens on the state. In addition, although we may as readers all recognise that the phrase takes part in a dominant ideology of motherhood which is essentially conservative, we may set that ideology within another framework of critique, that is, we may see this term critically and propose different forms of analysis for the same situation, preferring to refer to 'lone parents' or 'single mothers', which again entail a set of assumptions about the role of mothers and fathers but which do not foreground the fact of marriage as being the most salient feature, and do not necessarily propose that being single is a lack and is negative.

[24] R. Coward, *Female Desire: Women's Sexuality Today* (Paladin, London, 1984); and see Wareing, this volume.

[25] This is also the case for many songs addressing males, but the women's songs seem to take place in a wider ideological framework which makes those messages mean differently to the men's: for example there is no equivalent of Mills and Boon for men.

[26] As Bordo shows in her excellent article on anorexia nervosa and women's relation not only to food but to the notion of control (S. Bordo, 'Anorexia nervosa: psychopathology as the crystallisation of culture', in H. Crowley and S. Himmelweit, eds., op. cit. (1991). For Bordo, anorexia and other eating disorders are one way for women who are positioned as powerless and out of control to take control of one area of their lives – their intake of food and their body shape. Women are bombarded with images of what they are supposed to look like and their ideal image which obviously does not map onto their real image; even when the idealised ideological image is similar to the real body shape it is not perceived as such, since it is of course an ideological representation and cannot be mapped onto the real. Anorexia and other illnesses are ways of dealing with that gap between an ideal image which is constructed by society and the agency which women wield when they often do not have control in other areas of their lives. It is no coincidence that this is a phenomena which primarily affects adolescent girls who

control, where emotions take over and they 'fall' in love, without there being any active control over the process.[27] But like all ideologies, romantic love has at its heart a fundamental contradiction: it is about pleasure and enjoyment at the same time that it is based on suffering and despair. In the analysis which follows I would like to focus on this contradictory ideological position and consider what this means for an analysis of transitivity.

## An Analysis of a pop song

The pop song which I would like to analyse is one which was issued in 1992 by the Sugar Cubes and which is entitled *Hit*. Here is a sample of the lyrics [I have set out the song in lines which correspond to pauses within the song]:

1 This wasn't supposed to happen
2 I was happy by myself
3 Accidentally
4 you seduced me
5 I'm in love again

*Chorus*
6 I lie in my bed
7 Totally still
8 My eyes wide open
9 I'm in rapture
10 I don't believe this
11 I'm in love
12 Again

are just coming to terms with a range of ideological messages which often have conflicting messages about what they should be and look like. Bordo is not arguing that anorexia is a positive form of agency in relation to the powerlessness of adolescent females, but she does see that control and agency are crucial elements in this disorder.

[27] Consider for example, Karen Carpenter's 'I'll never fall in love again', which exposes the contradictory nature of romantic love for women: the female character states throughout the song that she will not fall in love again because love only means 'hurt' and 'sorrow'. Yet the song undermines itself when she states that she will not fall in love 'at least until tomorrow'. Thus, love is something which is to be avoided and yet which is also sought after because it is pleasurable.

13  This wasn't supposed to happen
14  I've been hit by your charm
15  How could you do this to me
16  I'm in love
17  Again

*Chorus*

The rest of the song is similar in sentiments and expression, except that a hard-edged male voice interrupts the reverie in a quite different key and voice quality stating:

1  I said ouch
2  This really hurts
3  This has been practised for millions of years
4  Therefore we are . . . guess what?
5  I'm a boy
6  You're a girl.

There are a number of points to make before beginning the analysis of the song. First, it is important not to forget the fact that this is a song and that the voice quality and the key in which the song has been written are important factors to the way in which it will be interpreted. A full analysis would consider the musical qualities of the song itself.[28] However, for the purposes of brevity, I will concentrate on voice quality because that is the most important analytical factor in relation to transitivity. Secondly, in contemporary pop songs the meanings and status of the actual words are subject to some debate; there are critics who feel that it is possible to analyse the words as if they were poetry;[29] and there are others who insist that this is not in fact necessarily the way that they are interpreted by listeners. Listeners may perform a 'slack' reading of the words, and not feel that they have to understand or even hear some of the words; the indistinctness of some words may in fact be part of the whole 'feel' and atmosphere of the song.[30] In this song, some of the words are unclear

[28] See B. Bradby, 'Do-talk and don't talk: the division of the subject in girl-group music', in S. Frith and A. Goodwin, eds., *On Record: A Rock and Pop Reader* (Routledge, London, 1990), pp. 341–368; B. Bradby and B. Torode, 'Pity Peggy Sue', in *Popular Music*, 4 (1984), pp. 183–206.
[29] See, for example, A. Day, *Joker Man: Reading the Lyrics of Bob Dylan* (Blackwell, Oxford, 1988).
[30] For example it may be an explicit reaction to earlier songs, particularly of

and they are not included in the record sleeve, so whether the words are as significant as they are in the analysis of lyric poetry is debatable. Thirdly, it must be remembered that there are a number of different readings available for any text. There has been much debate within cultural studies in particular about the meaning of artefacts: whether a critic can simply discover or uncover the real meaning of a particular text or whether in fact the meanings can only be found through consulting the people by whom that cultural artefact is used.[31] This is of particular significance in the discussion of transitivity, where it has been asserted in many of the analyses I have mentioned above that linguistic choices result in particular meanings. Finally, it must be remembered that pop songs are used in very specific ways; listeners have emotional investments in pop songs and tend to listen to them repeatedly. Pop music is particularly important for adolescents who use pop music as a way of constructing for themselves a sense of self and community. It is difficult to simply analyse these texts therefore as artefacts, since they have very tangible effects on listeners in the real world.[32]

The song itself is produced as a very modern song: it is not a conventional romantic song written in a major key and dominated by a strong melodic verse and chorus. Instead, the song opens in a minor key with discordant guitars and a very full sound; this signals to its listener that it is a 'modern' and hard-edged view of love. Nevertheless, as I will show, the view of love which is propounded in the song seems to be seriously at odds with the style of the backing and the singing itself. The beat of the song is fairly fast in contrast to the slow, drawn out singing style of the female vocalist, who sings in a very grainy and melancholic manner; the voice is produced in a highly emotional way, each syllable being stressed and stretched, even words like 'I' and 'this' being extended over several notes. The musical range of her singing is very restricted in the verses, ranging over only four

the 1950s where articulation of the words was crucial. For a discussion of meaning and song lyrics see S. Frith, 'Why do songs have words', in *Music for Pleasure; Essays in the Sociology of Pop Polity* (Oxford, 1988), pp. 105–128. For a more detailed analysis of slack readings, see Z. Wicomb, 'Motherhood and the surrogate reader: race, gender and interpretation', in S. Mills, ed., *Gendering the Reader* (Routledge, London, 1994).

[31] See S. Mills, ibid., for a fuller account.

[32] See J. Savage, 'The enemy within: sex, rock and identity', in S. Frith, *Facing the Music: Essays on Pop, Rock and Culture* (Mandarin, London, 1988), pp. 131–173.

notes, and the melody does not harmonise at all with the backing; furthermore, each phrase ends on a lower note, giving an overall melancholic feel to the song as a whole. The verse which is sung by the male singer is, by contrast, shouted or spoken in a very staccato style, rather than being sung. The voice quality of both singers has an effect on the way that the text is interpreted because it could be argued that the voice quality of the female singer sets up a framework within which we decide how to interpret the song; for example, we could decide that the voice quality has either a 'yearning' feel to it, which the female is enjoying, or that it is 'yearning' of despair and suffering.

Let us first of all analyse the transitivity choices within the text. The first phrase: 'this wasn't supposed to happen' (line 1) is a clear use of a transitivity choice where there is no agent: rather than someone acting – someone deciding to fall in love with someone else, something has happened. This puts the protagonist in the position of 'affected', that is, 'acted upon'; but it also means that her being in love has just 'happened' – it is not as if anyone has made a conscious decision. Romantic love is portrayed and experienced in this way in Western cultures but it should be stressed that there is nothing 'natural' about this form of representation.[33] Even this verb 'happen' is mediated through the use of 'supposed to', and because this is passivised, it is unclear whose emotions are being described. This initial clause seems very distanced and lacking in an agent. The protagonist could have stated 'I didn't want this to happen', but here the transitivity choice distances this level of decision-making from her. Her choice of 'this' is also interesting as a description of the process of being in love; the protagonist could have chosen to describe it using a verb (falling in love) or nominalisation, rather than the use of the objectifying 'this'. Thus, from the very beginning of the song, the protagonist is presented as not being in control.

This view of the protagonist is affirmed by other verbal choices, for example, 'Accidentally you seduced me', line 3/4. Here the woman is seen as the 'affected' participant, and there is another actor 'you' who seduces her. This verb is one which is traditionally reserved for male activity and it is a curious choice, since it seems to be quite an old-fashioned word with connotations of rakishness, where the male is the only one with sexual appetite and the female is simply the

[33] See Coward, op. cit. (1984).

recipient of male sexual action. 'Seduce' also has connotations of unwillingness on the part of the female, which affirms the sense from line 1 that the protagonist does not want this involvement.[34] However, the verb is mediated by the use of 'accidentally', which seems to conflict with the intentionality of the verb to seduce. Here, what is, on an initial analysis, a material action intention process is modified, so that it acts as a supervention process. We can interpret this clause in two ways: either the process by which she is 'seduced' is one where the male character is not necessarily in direct control either; or the male is portrayed as interpreting the relationship as 'a one night stand'.

The first verse thus seems to present a particular view of romantic love which is contradictory: we have a female character who is independent, since she was 'happy by myself' and she states clearly that she did not want or intend to fall in love again; the male character although portrayed as 'seducing' her, does so in a way which might suggest that he too did not wish this to happen. It is also interesting to note that this first verse signals that she does not see this as a once in a lifetime event since she states 'I'm in love again', in much the same way that one might state 'I've got the flu again'. The ideology of romantic love works on the notion that there is only one person with whom we will fall in love and that this will last for ever. The first verse seems to be both challenging this myth and proposing that romantic love is something which needs to be resisted.

The second verse also takes up this idea that falling in love is a nuisance, but suggests that it is something for which the male is responsible and which the woman resents. The second verse affirms the first in that here again the female actor takes the role of affected or recipient; she is the recipient of the passive clause 'I've been hit by your charm', (line 14). It is interesting that the verb 'hit' has been used here since this is an unusual collocative choice, being a much more violent verb than is generally used with 'charm'. It suggests that the protagonist had developed a certain protective barrier around herself when she was single which the male has broken down by seducing her. In line 15, she asks 'How could you do this to me?' where her role is again the 'affected participant'.

The other verses in the song have similar clauses where the female is positioned as the recipient of actions only or is the focus of passive

[34] See Hollway, op. cit. (1992), for a discussion of the discourses informing the discussion of male and female sexuality and emotions.

clauses where the male character is the agent. Thus, rather than romantic love being viewed as something to be welcomed, here it is seen as something which is imposed on the female and which she resents and resists.

However, there is a sense in which this slightly challenging view of romantic love is itself undercut by the chorus. There seems to be a clear break in meaning between the verses sung by the female character and the chorus, also sung by the female. This break is signalled to the listener by the move to a major key and a more upbeat tempo. The voice quality is less melancholic and seems to gain a certain clarity and strength. The transitivity choices are in line with those of the first and second verses, in that the protagonist does not act but experiences. However, line 9 'I'm in rapture' which describes a very positive, almost religious experience, creates a much more positive interpretative context. Because of this positive context we interpret 'I don't believe this' (line 10) to mean 'This is so good that I can hardly believe it is possible', rather that 'I don't believe this could happen to me because I was happy to be single'. We also interpret the statement 'I'm in love again' (lines 11/12) in a more positive way than when it occurred in the first and second verses. The chorus serves to present us with an image of the female character as passive, but enjoying that passivity; she does not act, she experiences: all of the clauses here are either mental processes ('I don't believe this') or material action processes which are intransitive: that is, they do not have an effect on another person or thing. Thus 'I lie in my bed' is intransitive in that it does not have an object; there is no affected participant. The verbs in other clauses in the chorus have been omitted, so that there are simple descriptive phrases like 'my eyes wide open' which describes the state of the female character without her acting.

Given that we have two contradictory views of romantic love here ('I don't want to be in love as I was happy to be single' and 'I enjoy being in love') it is surprising that listeners do in fact impose some coherence on the song as whole. This is partly due to the fact that the clauses are not related by co-ordination or subordination, but are hypotactic, that is they are related by contiguity, and the reader is forced to make some connection between them. Each of the clauses is free-standing. Hence, the logical and temporal relations between them have to be inferred by the reader. If the listener considers the ideology of romantic love to be self-evident or common-sense, she will make a logical connection between the potentially negative first verse and the chorus, that is between a representation of anxiety about being in love, and a representation of pleasure in being in love. She will therefore reconcile the contradictions: namely, love is a nuisance and love is blissful. If the listener is critical of this ideology where suffering in being seduced and pleasure in being in love are the same, then she will find it difficult to make this transition. For those who are critical of romantic love, this pleasure in suffering can only be seen as a form of masochism, the pleasures of being acted upon and being passive.

The male verse is a further contradictory element in this song; as I mentioned earlier, the verse is marked off from the rest of the song by voice quality, singing style, tempo and key. It is in marked contrast to the female's views, since it seems to be proposing that this form of masochism entailed in romantic love is 'natural', since it 'has been practised for millions of years' (line 3) and is inevitable simply because there are 'boys' and 'girls'. The male does not comment on his 'accidental seduction' of the female, but seems here to be suffering in a similar manner to the female; he does not foreground his agency here, using instead a passive 'this has been practised' (line 3) and a seeming intransitive verb 'this really hurts' (line 2), where the affected participant is understood to be 'this really hurts *me*'.

We might also consider the way that the text as a whole addresses listeners, since these transitivity choices do not take place in a vacuum but in relation to a listener who interprets them. So, for example, we need to consider the ways in which listeners are called upon or co-opted to align themselves with the statements which are made in the text. Some pop songs call on them in quite explicit ways to agree to certain statements, through direct address, that is, through the use of pronouns such as 'you' and 'I', where the listener accepts these pronouns as referring to herself.[35] Within this song, there is very little overt reader positioning, because 'you' is not used in a way in

---

[35] If you take as an example Mungo Jerry's song *In the Summertime*, which contains the lines 'In the summertime when the weather is high, you can reach right up and touch the sky' the 'you' is the same one which assents to later statements where 'in the summertime, you've got women, you've got women on your mind'. Because of the curious nature of the pronouns 'you' and 'I' and also because of specific ways of interpreting pop songs, they can refer to both the addressee of the song, the fictional person to whom the song is addressed, as well as the listener. The listener in both cases sees that the 'you' is supposed to refer to herself, and can either assent or resist the indirect address which assumes that the listener is male and indeed has 'women on your mind'.

which it could be addressed to the reader. It is used exclusively for the fictional character who is the absent lover. 'I', however, is thematised, i.e. put in the position of the most important part of the clause, in very many of the sentences. Listeners have the option of merging the 'I' of themselves with the 'I' of the song, and seeing, indirectly, similarities or differences between the two. Most of the address in this song is of an indirect kind, where the listener has to actively work at generating meanings from the text.

As I mentioned above, Burton has developed ways of challenging the representation of women as passive, and one of them is to rewrite the text using different transitivity choices; this has a dual function – it can serve to highlight the choices which seem in some ways self-evident, and it can lead the listener to think in different ways about action and agency. Thus, a rewriting of the transitivity choices, following Burton (op. cit.) in this song would highlight the fact that the female character is essentially passive and this can lead to an analysis whereby it is clear that the ideology of romantic love has difficulty in accommodating the notion of women as agents. This does not lead to a 'politically correct' view of love, that is, one where women are not represented as the victims, but rather, simply highlights the fact that within representations of romantic love, there are often roles carved out for women which seem natural and which result in women being viewed as 'naturally' passive and acted upon. In the process of rewriting this text, for example, we would see the impossibility of making the actions of the female all 'material action intention' within this type of ideology; for example, statements such as 'I hit you with my charm' or 'I seduced you' do not make sense within the ideological framework within which the song is set. Similarly, representations of romantic love function from the point of view of the female in general and the male is not fleshed out in such detail or is, as here, almost completely absent: we might consider rewriting some of the passive clauses so that the male's actions are heightened by the active voice; for example 'Accidentally I seduced you'; 'I hit you with my charm' and 'How could I do this to you?' We do not know from the song whether the male character is similarly 'in rapture' and lying on his bed thinking about her or whether he has simply seduced her and is now busy seducing someone else, or has his mind on other things, for example, work or leisure.

One feminist interpretation of this song, following Burton, would see the woman character as a victim of male 'seduction' who is turned into a passive character through the male actions; the male would be seen as a powerful figure whereas the woman is the powerless figure. This type of analysis would count up the number of choices within certain transitivity categories and show that there was a clear correlation between the choice of the passive/affected role, the use of intransitive verbs, the concentration on mental processes and a more general position of lack of control and agency.

Whilst this type of analysis would probably form the basis for any interpretation, it is clearly not adequate to describe some of the complexities of this song, as I have shown above. The meaning of the song is not a simple question of adding up the number of clause types. A more complex analysis would see the song and these transitivity choices as a representation which displays some of the contradictions in romantic love, and would see that the song can also be seen to be demonstrating some of the tensions that exist at present around love: this would acknowledge the pleasures associated with passivity and with being the acted-upon rather than the agent, as well as acknowledging the wish not to be passive and acted upon. It would also see power as more a relation than an imposition, that is, it is difficult to see here who is in control. From one reading position, we can see the absent male as in control, and the female as simply the acted-upon: she is dependent on his actions; but in another reading we can see the male as almost irrelevant: he seduced her (accidentally) but she is the one who is now in control since she has adopted the ideology of romantic love, and she is after all 'in rapture' although perhaps no longer 'happy', as she was when she was single (line 2). This type of analysis calls for a recognition of the contradictions and pleasures of romantic love, and foregrounds the fact that perhaps being acted upon may be pleasurable but dangerous. It also calls for a recognition that ideologies are not static and are frequently called into crisis.

What often happens in feminist transitivity analysis is that there is a simple replication of the message 'all texts about and by women contain these representations of passivity'. What I am trying to foreground here is that making sense of texts is in fact much more complicated: this text does indeed contain some evidence of the female as passive and as acted upon; however, this analysis alone does not show the contradictory elements that are contained within the text – that being in love is pleasurable, that being in love is not pleasurable. The song does not present these positions as contradictory but tries to mask this by presenting them as if they make sense. What my analysis has tried to show is the fact that these choices are contradictory. Listeners to this song have choices to make, in that they have to decide whether they will accept the contradictions within the song, or whether they will in fact only selectively listen to the song: for example, reading only those sections of the text which add up to the message 'romantic love is enjoyable' or those which add up to 'romantic love is a nuisance'.

Listeners may feel that these contradictions are so great that they listen to the song critically, or finally listen to some other kind of song. But what this analysis is aware of is that ideology is not simply a representation of a single position, but rather that it may represent a more complex vision of itself in crisis; and also showing the great pleasures invested in this type of representation, as well as the more negative aspects. Listeners may find pleasure in aligning themselves to the partial representations of women as passive even at the same time that they do not generally see themselves or other women in this way.

Feminist anaylsis of this sort is not concerned necessarily with proposing that this type of song is 'wrong', since it does not see its meaning as singular or univocal, and therefore does not propose, as in the 1960s, that we should not listen to certain types of music or read certain types of text. But, rather it is concerned with highlighting the fact that for many women, some forms of pleasure may be concerned with not being an agent, but that this is set within more critical discourses which recognise that we would be happier in control or 'by myself'.

Sandra Harding states that this more complex analysis may be a direction in which feminist theory should go, rather than opting for a simpler form of analysis which sees a particular type of representation as right or wrong. She says:

> Instead of fidelity to the assumption that coherent theory is a desirable end in itself and the only reliable guide to action, we can take as our standard fidelity to *parameters* of dissonance within and between assumptions of patriarchal discourses. This approach to theorising captures what some take to be a distinctively women's emphasis on contextual thinking and decision-making and on the processes necessary for gaining understanding in a world not of our own making – that is, a world that does not encourage us to fantasise about how we could order reality into the forms we desire. It locates the ways in which a valuably 'alienated consciousness' 'bifurcated consciousness', 'oppositional consciousness' might function at the level of active theory-making – as well as at the level of scepticism and rebellion. We need to be able to cherish certain kinds of intellectual, political and psychic discomforts, to see as

inappropriate and even self-defeating certain kinds of clear solutions to the problems we have been posing.[36]

Although Harding's views were formulated in a discussion of feminist theory as a whole, I have quoted them at length here because of their relevance as to how to make sense and interpret the text by the Sugar Cubes. If we adhere to the principal of feminist analysis being a clear cut critique of the ways that women have been represented, then we will offer a reading of this text which is unequivocal and which sees the meaning of the transitivity choices all pointing in one direction. The female character is passive; the transitivity choices are of particular types, and this has some impact on the fact that the woman is represented as passive. We would then go on to argue that this is a general case for representations of women as a whole, and perhaps demand that this situation change.

With a more complex model which Harding is proposing, we are able to see that whilst this analysis is correct on one level, it does not explain the power that these types of representations have for women listeners and the reasons why women in particular are subject to this type of representational practice; nor is it aware of the other messages in the text which undercut this dominant passive role for the female character. This more complex form of feminist analysis would set out to explore the way that passivity is constructed as pleasurable, and at the same time analyse the ways that the text displays a number of contradictory forces, which undercut and challenge that pleasure; for example, showing the way that the female character was 'happy' on her own, and in fact does not want or need this type of disruption to her life.

Thus, analysis of transitivity is an excellent basis for interpretation, but only when we acknowledge that transitivity like other linguistic features can mean in a variety of different ways, according to the type of context in which it is set and also according to the set of assumptions which the reader brings to bear on the interpretive process. The interpretations of text which we can make using this more complex model of feminist analysis are perhaps less clear-cut and are certainly less satisfying, but in some senses they do approximate more to the complexity of the processes whereby we make sense of ideological representations.

[36] S. Harding, 'The instability of the analytical categories of feminist theory', in H. Crowley and S. Himmelweit, eds. (op. cit., 1992), p. 342.

# Notes on Contributors

**ara Calvo** teaches in the Department of English at the University of ranada. Her main research interests include stylistics and Renaissance ama, areas on which she has published several articles. She is currently orking on the stylistics of feminist crime fiction.

**sley Jeffries** lectures on English language and stylistics in the School of umanities and Music at the University of Huddersfield. She recently pubhed *The Language of Twentieth Century Poetry* (Macmillan, 1993).

**arion Lomax** is a Senior Lecturer in English at St Mary's College, rawberry Hill, University of Surrey. Her main publications are *Stage Images d Traditions: Shakespeare to Ford* (Cambridge University Press, 1987); *The epshow Girl* (Bloodaxe, 1989); and *Beyond Men and Dreams*, a chamber era for the Royal Opera House Garden Venture, was performed in 1991. ie is also editor of four plays by John Ford (Oxford University Press, 1995) d is currently editing *The Rover* by Aphra Behn (New Mermaids).

**ira Mills** is a Senior Lecturer in linguistics and critical theory in the epartment of English and Drama at the University of Loughborough. She -wrote *Feminist Readings/Feminists Reading* (Harvester, 1989) and *Ways of ading* (Routledge, 1992). Her book on *Discourses of Difference: Women's avel Writing and Imperialism* appeared also in 1992 for Routledge. She is rrently working on *Feminist Stylistics* for Routledge, and editing a collecon of essays on *Language and Gender* for Longman.

**ouise Sylvester** is a Research Associate at King's College London, and a siting lecturer at the Roehampton Institute. She has published articles on haucer, and on feminism and Jewish identity. Her book *Studies in the xical Field of Expectation* will be published in 1994 (Rodopi).

**nne Varty** is a lecturer in both the Departments of English and Drama, at byal Holloway University of London. Her main research interests include rindberg, Ibsen, Aestheticism and Pater (she is bibliographer for *The Pater ewsletter*). She is the co-editor of *Liz Lockhead's Voices* (Edinburgh Univery Press, 1993).

**atie Wales** is a Reader in English Language at Royal Holloway University London. Her main publications are *A Dictionary of Stylistics* (Longman, 89) and *The Language of James Joyce* (Macmillan, 1992). She is currently orking on a book for Cambridge University Press on English pronouns. She currently Chair of The Poetics and Linguistics Association (PALA), and sistant editor of the journal *Language and Literature* (Longman).

**ian Wareing** is a lecturer in English language and linguistics at the behampton Institute, and recently a visiting lecturer at Michigan State niversity. She has published several articles on stylistics, gender and classom interaction, the subject of her nearly-completed Ph.D thesis.

157